The
EVERYTHING®
GERMAN
PHRASE
BOOK
—— and ——
Dictionary

D0054676

EDWARD SWICK, MA

THE
EVERYTHING®
Series

Dear Reader,

Danke schön! Thanks for choosing *The Everything® German Phrase Book and Dictionary* as your vehicle for learning or brushing up on your German. I think you're going to find it easy to use and the perfect companion for a journey into the German culture and German language. Keep it in a pocket and handy for those important moments when you have to express yourself in your new language.

My long-held interest in German is no mystery. Some in my family came from Germany, so I had the advantage of hearing the language from childhood. When I began my formal study of German, I realized my interest in it was the fundamental part of my future profession, and I ended up in graduate school in Hamburg. That marvelous city became my second home and my base for adventures into other areas of Germany. After I became a teacher of German in the United States, I never lost the need to travel back to my second home and became acquainted with every region of Germany, Austria, and Switzerland. Although German is used in all three countries, there are some differences; most differences are in pronunciation, but sometimes even regional vocabulary words are used to describe the same thing.

My hope is that this book will help guide you in discovering the wonderful things and friendly people that the German-speaking countries of Europe have to offer.

Don't be afraid to experiment with your new language. Make comments about the wonderful sights you'll see. Or just ask questions. You're going to be surprised how many smiles you'll earn when you approach a shopkeeper or passerby with one of your German phrases.

Have fun learning. *Viel Spaß!*

Edward Swick

The EVERYTHING® Series

These handy, accessible books give you all you need to tackle a difficult project, gain a new hobby, or even brush up on something you learned back in school but have since forgotten. You can read from cover to cover or just pick out information from our four useful boxes.

 Alerts: Urgent warnings

 Essentials: Quick handy tips

Facts: Important snippets of information

Questions: Answers to common questions

When you're done reading, you can finally say you know **EVERYTHING®**!

PUBLISHER Karen Cooper

MANAGING EDITOR, EVERYTHING SERIES Lisa Laing

COPY CHIEF Casey Ebert

ASSISTANT PRODUCTION EDITOR Alex Guarco

ACQUISITIONS EDITOR Brett Palana-Shanahan

SENIOR DEVELOPMENT EDITOR Brett Palana-Shanahan

EVERYTHING® SERIES COVER DESIGNER Erin Alexander

Visit the entire Everything® series at *www.everything.com*

THE
EVERYTHING®
GERMAN
PHRASE
BOOK
—— and ——
Dictionary

Edward Swick, MA

Adams Media
New York London Toronto Sydney New Delhi

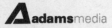

Adams Media
An Imprint of Simon & Schuster, Inc.
57 Littlefield Street
Avon, Massachusetts 02322

An Everything® Series Book.
Everything® and everything.com® are registered trademarks of Simon & Schuster, Inc.

ADAMS MEDIA and colophon are trademarks of Simon and Schuster.

For information about special discounts for bulk purchases, please contact Simon & Schuster Special Sales at 1-866-506-1949 or business@simonandschuster.com.

The Simon & Schuster Speakers Bureau can bring authors to your live event. For
more information or to book an event contact the Simon & Schuster Speakers
Bureau at 1-866-248-3049 or visit our website at www.simonspeakers.com.

Manufactured in the United States of America

10 9 8 7 6 5 4

Library of Congress Cataloging-in-Publication Data has been applied for.

ISBN 978-1-4405-9308-6
ISBN 978-1-4405-9309-3(ebook)

Acknowledgments

With much gratitude to Stefan Feyen
for all his help and suggestions.

Contents

Contents

The Top 10 German Phrases You Should Know

1. **Do you speak English?** *Sprechen Sie Englisch?*
   (SHPREHCH en zee ENG lish)
2. **Hello.** *Guten Tag.*
   (GOO ten tuck)
3. **Goodbye.** *Auf Wiedersehen.*
   (owf VEE duh zay en)
4. **My name is . . .** *Ich heiße . . .*
   (eech HICE eh)
5. **Where is . . . ?** *Wo ist . . . ?*
   (voe ist)
6. **How much does it cost?** Wie viel kostet es?
   (vee feel KAWS tet ess)
7. **I have . . .** *Ich habe . . .*
   (eech HAH beh)
8. **I don't have any . . .** *Ich habe kein . . .*
   (eech HAH beh kine)
9. **I need . . .** *Ich brauche . . .*
   (eech BROWCH eh)
10. **I would like . . .** *Ich möchte . . .*
    (eech MERCH teh)

Introduction

It's never too late to learn a new language. But there is one prerequisite, which apparently you have, because you're reading this book: You need interest in the subject! Only you know exactly why you're interested in German. Perhaps a relative came from Germany years ago and you want to visit the site of your family's origins. Or maybe you just want to travel for fun or business and be able to communicate with the natives. It doesn't really matter what your reason is. What matters is that you have the interest, and that's the initial key to success.

Being able to communicate in German will open doors for you that most non-German-speaking travelers never even know exist. You can experience the native culture because culture and language are interrelated. Knowing what the street signs and advertisements mean, being able to read the headlines of a newspaper, understanding what the butcher is recommending to the customer next to you—these are things that only a German-speaking traveler can do. And *The Everything*® *German Phrase Book and Dictionary* can provide you with the phrases and vocabulary that will give you the basic skills to do just that.

Naturally, just carrying this book around with you won't do the trick. You have to study the phrases and practice them. And remember that language—whether German, English, Russian, or Japanese—is first and foremost a spoken entity. You have to speak. You have to practice your phrases out loud. Just thinking them or reading them to yourself won't do. Languages are spoken.

German is used in other countries besides Germany. It is the official language of Austria, and it is a primary language of Switzerland and Liechtenstein. It certainly is no surprise that there are large German-speaking communities in the United States and Canada. Immigration from the German-speaking world in the last two centuries occurred on a large scale, so many North Americans speak or understand German. Since German is used in different regions, there are regional differences of pronunciation and vocabulary usage. For example, in English, someone in the south of the United States might say "skillet" while someone in the north might use the phrase "frying pan." In some English-speaking regions, you say "I'll wait for you." In other regions, you say, "I'll wait on you." Variations like this also occur in the German language. However, there is a standard German language that is generally accepted in all German-speaking regions, and that is the language used in *The Everything® German Phrase Book and Dictionary.*

Many foreign words have entered the German language in the past two decades. This is particularly true about English words. English words that are used frequently in German are provided throughout this book. For example, the German word for "basketball" is

Basketball. You're going to be surprised just how many "German" words you already know.

Recently, the experts on the German language revised the rules for German spelling. Don't worry. That won't cause you a problem, because German spelling is for the most part phonetic. What the experts did was standardize a few letter combinations that differed depending upon the region in which they were used and depending upon the generation of the person who used them. For example, the German letter *ß* is sometimes replaced by *ss*, because they have the same pronunciation. But some people preferred *ß* and others preferred *ss*. So now there's a rule: If the vowel sound that precedes these letters is long, use *ß*. If it's short, use *ss*. Therefore, the word *weiß* ("white," pronounced "vice") is spelled with *ß*, because the vowel is long. The word *dass* ("that," pronounced "duss") is spelled with *ss*, because the vowel is short.

The three main sections of *The Everything® German Phrase Book and Dictionary* are the lessons, the phrases, and the appendices. Naturally, you should start with the lessons, which provide you with the basics of grammar and pronunciation as well as practical phrases. Chapter 1 introduces you to the German language and how it is both similar to and different from English. Chapter 2 provides you with the fundamentals of German grammar and structure. With a careful reading of these two chapters, you will have a basic understanding of German that will help to guide you through the other chapters.

Chapters 3 through 14 provide you with practical German phrases for a variety of situations. Each phrase is accompanied by its English equivalent translation (not all phrases can be translated word for word) and by the approximate English pronunciation of the German phrase. When there is no equivalent English pronunciation of a German sound, the English sound closest to it is provided. An explanation of this is found in Chapter 1.

There are two appendices at the end of the book: a German/English dictionary and an English/German dictionary. These will come in handy when you need the translation of a specific word.

The Everything® German Phrase Book and Dictionary is a handy vehicle for learning German. It not only provides you with the most important grammatical functions of the language and a simple guide to German pronunciation, but it also offers practical phrases for travel, shopping, dining, and business. With that said, it's time to begin.

Good luck! *Viel Glück!*

Chapter 1

Introduction to German

German is one of the Germanic languages of Europe and a close relative to English. German and English are brother and sister languages that were separated by time and geography during the migrations of the Anglo-Saxons. This means you can find many similarities of vocabulary and structure in the two languages. That's important: It makes learning German just a little bit easier. Some important facts about German will be introduced here, which will give you a basis for understanding the nature of the German language and what it will entail to learn to use it effectively.

Reading German

Just like English, German uses the twenty-six-letter alphabet designed by the Romans. Although most of the letters are the same visually, some have a distinctly unique pronunciation in German. Learning the German sounds of the alphabet is not a difficult task and will allow you to read words with ease.

 Fact

> In addition to the letters that are identical in both German and English, there are four letters that occur in German that do not in English. Three require the addition of an umlaut over a vowel: ä, ö, and ü. The fourth letter is a special compound of s and z and looks like this in the modern language: ß.

Once you are familiar with the characteristics of German pronunciation, you will find that you can pronounce nearly all words upon seeing them for the first time, because German is, for the most part, a phonetic language. Any variances from standard pronunciation will be pointed out and explained. In the following Pronunciation Key you will find examples of how to pronounce individual letters, letter combinations, and special letters. The comparable English pronunciation of the letters and letter combinations is only a guide. To be absolutely precise about pronunciation, ask a German-speaking friend to say the sounds for you. However, the key will provide you with a close facsimile of German that will be understood by any German speaker.

Pronunciation Key

German	English Representation Letter(s)	Comparable English Pronunciation
A	a	"a" in father
Ä	ay	"ai" in pain
AA	a	"a" in father
AI	i	"i" in like
AH	a	"a" in father
AU	ow	"ow" in how
ÄU	oy	"oy" in boy
B	b	"b" in baby
C	ts	"ts" in its
CH	h	"ch" in Scottish loch
CK	k	"ck" in sick
D	d	"d" in dad
DT	t	"t" in tot
E	ay	"ai" in pain
EH	ay	"ai" in pain
EI	i	"i" in like
EU	oy	"oy" in boy
F	f	"f" in fife
G	g	"g" in go
H	h	"h" in how
I	ee	"ee" in sleep
IE	ee	"ee" in sleep
J	y	"y" in yolk
K	k	"k" in kick
L	l	"l" in lull

M	m	"m" in mom
N	n	"n" in nun
O	o	"o" in open
OH	o	"o" in open
OO	o	"o" in open
Ö	er	"e" in her
P	p	"p" in pup
PF	pf	"pf" in carp food
PH	f	"ph" in photo
QU	kv	"kv" in sick vet
R	r	"r" in red (guttural)
ER	er	"er" in father (British)
S	z	"z" in zoo
S	s	(final) "s" in kiss
SS	s	"ss" in kiss
ß	s	"ss" in kiss
SCH	sh	"sh" in shush
T	t	"t" in tot
TSCH	ch	"ch" in church
TZ	ts	"ts" in its
U	oo	"oo" in moon
UH	oo	"oo" in moon
Ü	(ue)	("oo" while saying "ee")
V	f	"f" in fife
	v	"v" in very
W	v	"v" in very
X	x	"x" six
Y	(ue)	("oo" while saying "ee")
Z	ts	"ts" in its

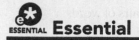

Essential

> Certain consonants that end a word and sometimes a syllable become voiceless. When a consonant is voiced there is resonation in the throat (*b, g, z,* and so on). When it is voiceless, there is no resonation in the throat. The German voiced consonants are *d, g, w,* and *z.* Their voiceless counterparts are *p, t, k, f,* and *s.*

Vowels

Pronouncing German vowels typically does not come easy to people who are used to speaking English. A few simple rules and some practice will make it easier.

Umlaut Vowels

Only three vowels can add an umlaut: *a, o,* and *u.* The umlaut is a signal that the sound of the vowel has been altered. In the case of *a* ("a" in father), the vowel *ä* is pronounced similar to the German letter *e* ("ai" in pain). When *o* adds an umlaut, it signals a new sound that does not entirely exist in English. The vowel *ö* is much like the *e* in the English word "her." In making this sound, omit the *h* and the *r* and retain the sound of the vowel *e.* When you add an umlaut to *u,* you have a sound that does not occur in English. The vowel sound *ü* can be produced by pursing the lips to say the English sound *oo* (as in moon) but simultaneously pronouncing the English sound *ee* (as in seen).

Practice saying the following pairs of words.

bar	*Bär*
schon	*schön*
fuhr	*für*

Note: Because there is no English equivalent of the sounds *ö* and *ü*, they will be represented in the chapters that follow by "er" and "ue" when the phonetic pronunciation is shown. In addition, the stressed syllable in a word will appear in capital letters: *Vater* (FAH tuh).

Short and Long Vowels

The vowels can be pronounced as either "short" vowels or "long" vowels. Short vowels tend to precede a double consonant, and long vowels tend to precede a single consonant. Look at the following examples and their pronunciation.

Short Vowels	Long Vowels
Gasse ("a" in what)	*Gas* ("a" in father)
fällen ("e" in get)	*Käse* ("ai" in pain)
Kette ("e" in get)	*geben* ("ai" in pain)
Ross ("o" in toss)	*los* ("o" in open)
können ("er" short *e* in her)	*schön* ("er" long *e* in her)
Butter ("oo" in look)	*tun* ("oo" in moon)
müssen	*spülen*
("eu" short *oo* with *e*-sound)	("eu" long *oo* with *e*-sound)

Consonants

German uses pronunciations and consonant combinations that are unfamiliar to native English speakers.

The Consonant Combination *Ch*

This consonant combination is often imitated by English speakers by the sounds *k* or *sh*. But it is really neither of those. To form the German *ch*, pronounce the sound *k* but open the throat slightly to permit a raspy rush of air to be exhaled. This requires considerable practice for English speakers—except for the Scottish, who have a similar sound in Scottish words such as *loch*, which means "lake."

Practice saying the following words.

- *ich*
- *ach*
- *hoch*
- *such*

The Letter *R*

The German letter *r* is pronounced in two different ways, depending upon the geographical region. The German language is used not only in Germany, but also in Austria, Switzerland, and Liechtenstein. In some areas, particularly in the south, the sound *r* is a rolled *r* as heard in Italian or Russian. This sound is made by "flapping" a *d* on the palate of the mouth with the tongue.

The second *r* is often more difficult for English speakers. This sound is made at the back of the throat where the German *ch* sound is made. Pronounce the *ch* sound and hold the final aspiration (a raspy rush of exhaled air). The point where that sound is made is where the German *r* is made. Without moving the jaw, change the sound *ch* to *r* by saying "ra." This can be done by slowly saying "ach ra." To become proficient using this sound will require regular practice, but in time you will find that you are using both the *ch* and the German *r* comfortably.

Many German words end in *er*. This combination of letters is similar to the final *er* in an English word as it is pronounced in Britain; for example, "father" is pronounced more like *fath-uh*. This British *er* is similar to the German final *er*.

Practice saying the following words.

rot	*Ring*
dort	*Karl*
Mutter	*Bruder*

The Letter Z

English has the sound of the German *z* at the end of words or syllables, but in English it is most often written as *ts* or *tz*. In German the final *z* is pronounced in the same way. The German word for "felt" is *Filz* and is pronounced "filts." This sound can also occur in the middle of a word; for example: *heizen*, pronounced "hytsen," which means "to heat." Unlike English, German also uses this sound to begin words. For example, *Zelt* is pronounced "tselt" and means "tent." The combination *tz* also exists in German, but it is found only at the end of words or between syllables; for example: *Fritz*, a name, and *blitzen*, "to flash lightning."

Practice saying the following words.

Zeit	*Zoo*
Harz	*Hitze*

The Letter Combinations *Sp* and *St*

The letter combinations *sp* and *st* have a unique pronunciation, especially when they begin a word or syllable. They are pronounced as if they begin with *sh*. Therefore, *Sport* is pronounced as "shport." *Stein* is pronounced as "shtine."

Practice saying the following words.

Spende	*sprich*
Stil	*Stadt*

German Dialects

Just like English, German has regional differences not only of pronunciation but also of vocabulary. In English, for example, whether you will say "corn on the cob" or "roasting ears" depends upon where you live. The same occurs in German vocabulary as well as in pronunciation. In the north of Germany near Hamburg, for example, it is common to hear the letter combinations *sp* and *st* pronounced differently than in the rest of Germany: The *sh* sound is not used; therefore, *Sport* is pronounced "sport" and *Stein* is pronounced "stine."

Contractions

German contractions occur when combining a preposition and a definite article. However, an apostrophe is not used in contractions; for example, *in das* (in the) becomes *ins*, *zu der* (to the) becomes *zur*, and *von dem* (from the) becomes *vom*.

Common Contractions

an das	*ans*	at the, or to the
an dem	*am*	at the
auf das	*aufs*	on the
in dem	*im*	in the
zu dem	*zum*	to the
bei dem	*beim*	by the
für das	*fürs*	for the
um das	*ums*	around the

Apostrophes are used in German to show that a letter has been left out of a word. A common expression that illustrates this is *wie geht's*, which asks "how are you?" In this expression the letter *e* has been dropped from the word *es* and replaced by an apostrophe.

Capitalization

German and English differ somewhat in how they capitalize nouns and adjectives. In German, all nouns are capitalized whether they are proper or common. The adjectives of proper nouns are not capitalized unless they are in an official name or title. Let's look at some examples:

Common Noun	English
Haus	house
Land	country
Schwester	sister

Proper Noun	Adjective	English
Amerika	*amerikanisch*	America/American
Deutschland	*deutsch*	Germany/German
England	*englisch*	England/English

Cognates

Cognates are words that are identical in both German and English (and often in other languages). Sometimes they are identical except for a letter change that is characteristic of the language. For example, *korrekt* is the German version of "correct" and uses the letter *k* where in English a *c* is used. If the German used *c*, the word would be pronounced radically differently. Look at the following list of cognates and take note of the German words that have a change of a letter to conform to German pronunciation.

Noun	Adjective
Automobil	*abstrakt*
Akzent	*aktiv*
Artist	*blind*
Baby	*effektiv*
Chance	*fair*
Elefant	*historisch*
Diplomat	*innovativ*
Hardware	*kommunistisch*
Kapitalist	*kritisch*
Konferenz	*lyrisch*
Manager	*mechanisch*
Name	*national*

Optimist	*negativ*
Party	*offensiv*
Pessimist	*politisch*
Pilot	*positiv*
Präsident	*relativ*
Problem	*rhythmisch*
Professor	*romantisch*
Restaurant	*solid*
Service	*sozialistisch*
Statistik	*strikt*
System	*total*

Can you guess the English meaning of the following words?

Familie	*Gitarre*
Natur	*perfekt*
attraktiv	*nervös*
Kaffee	*populär*

Patterns of Cognates

Certain cognates occur in groups that conform to patterns. Two large groups of such English words are nouns that end in *–ion* and *–y*. Another large category is a group of English adjectives that end in *–ic* or *–ical*. In German, the endings for these cognates are *–ion*, *–ie*, and *–isch*.

Nouns Ending in *–ion*	**Nouns Ending in *– ie***	**Adjectives Ending in *–isch***
Aversion	*Astronomie*	*astronomisch*
Dekoration	*Harmonie*	*harmonisch*
Formation	*Anatomie*	*anatomisch*

Information	*Psychiatrie*	*psychiatrisch*
Inspektion	*Kolonie*	*bibliographisch*
Koalition	*Fotografie*	*fotografisch*
Konstitution	*Epidemie*	*epidemisch*
Position	*Philosophie*	*philosophisch*
Reservation	*Biologie*	*biologisch*
Revolution	*Geographie*	*geographisch*
Situation	*Psychologie*	*psychologisch*
Spekulation	*Therapie*	*therapeutisch*
Tradition	*Melodie*	*melodisch*
Ventilation	*Geologie*	*geologisch*
Vibration	*Archäologie*	*archäologisch*

 **Question**

How do I know whether I'm pronouncing German words correctly?

By using this guide, you can pronounce German words in such a way that German speakers will understand you. To develop a good accent, you should take a class, purchase some audio tools, or work with a native speaker.

Words Common to German and English

Since German and English are languages in the same Germanic group, they have many words in common. Some are almost identical and have an identical meaning in both languages. Others have a slight spelling difference, and still others are used for completely different meanings in the two languages and often are similar only in the smallest of degrees. Let's look at some examples.

People

German	Comparable English	Modern English
Bruder	brother	brother
Gärtner	gardener	gardener
Knabe	knave	boy, lad
Mann	man	man, husband
Mutter	mother	mother
Onkel	uncle	uncle
Schwester	sister	sister
Sohn	son	son
Tochter	daughter	daughter
Vater	father	father

Animals

German	Comparable English	Modern English
Affe	ape	ape, monkey
Frosch	frog	frog
Kalb	calf	calf
Kuh	cow	cow
Lamm	lamb	lamb
Maus	mouse	mouse
Schaf	sheep	sheep
Schwein	swine	swine, pig
Spinne	spinner	spider
Ratte	rat	rat
Tier	deer	animal

Colors

German	Modern English
blau	blue
braun	brown
grau	gray
grün	green
rot	red
weiß	white

Miscellaneous

German	Modern English
alt	old
Arm	arm
beginn	begin
bei	by
Brot	bread
Feld	field
fett	fat
Finger	finger
frisch	fresh
Fuß	foot
Grab	grave
gut	good
halt	hold
hart	hard
Haus	house
ist	is
jung	young
kalt	cold

komm	come
mach	make
Milch	milk
Mond	moon
sing	sing
Sonne	sun
wann	when
warm	warm
Wetter	weather
Wolle	wool

Chapter 2

German Grammar Basics

This book provides ready-to-use lists of vocabulary and phrases for every situation. But still it's important to know why you're saying something in a specific way, so you can reuse a phrase in a new form that conforms to a new situation. This chapter is an introduction to the basics of German grammar. Grammatical structures will be explained and examples provided to illustrate how those structures function. When you finish these mini-lessons, you will have the basic skills for saying things in German with accuracy.

Names and Nouns

Just like English names, German names tend to refer to either males or females. As time goes by, some names are used less and less frequently because they are considered old-fashioned. At other times, new names become popular because they are the latest fad. But all in all, there are certain German names that are traditional and retain their popularity for long periods. Let's look at some traditional male German names.

Friedrich	*Helmut*	*Hermann*	*Johann*
Karl	*Reinhardt*	*Wolfgang*	

Here are some traditional names for females.

Charlotte	*Gretchen*	*Helga*	*Ingrid*
Klara	*Luise*	*Marianne*	

Just like English, German has trends in names. Some of the most popular first names for men and women come from foreign sources.

Boris	*Addy*
Lars	*Dagmar*
Terry	*Selma*

Surnames

When using a person's surname, you should precede it by the title *Herr* (Mr.) for a man and *Frau* (Mrs., Ms.) for a woman.

Herr Schneider	*Herr Braun*
Frau Benz	*Frau Keller*

Fact

> The title *Fräulein* (Miss) was used quite commonly in the past to refer to a single woman. But just as the women's movement created cultural changes in the English-speaking world, so too did those changes occur in Germany. It is now taboo to use *Fräulein*. All women are addressed by *Frau*.

Professional titles are used much the same in German as in English. They do not usually identify the gender of the person addressed (e.g., *Professor Schmidt, Doktor Brenner*).

When speaking to a professional, the titles *Herr* and *Frau* are used when the last name is omitted and the gender of the person is identified.

Herr Professor	*Frau Professor*
Frau Doktor	*Herr Lehrer* (teacher)

Nouns and Gender

Nouns are words that represent a person, an object, or even an idea or concept. "Boy," "pencil," and "education" are examples of nouns. In English, the gender of a noun is masculine if it refers to males, feminine if it refers to females, and neuter if it refers to inanimate objects. German is somewhat different. Many nouns that refer to males and females are masculine and feminine respectively. But many other nouns that refer to inanimate objects are masculine or feminine, and still other nouns that refer to living people are neuter. For example, *Mann* (man) and *Stuhl* (chair) are masculine. *Frau* (woman) and *Lampe* (lamp) are feminine. *Kind* (child) and *Haus* (house) are neuter.

It is important to know the gender of nouns. Gender determines how articles and adjectives are used with those nouns. It is wise to try to memorize the gender of a noun as you learn it. However, if you make a mistake and use the wrong gender, German speakers will still understand you and it won't be considered a major blunder.

It is often the form of a noun that determines its gender. Certain endings tend to signal a specific gender. For example, nouns that end in *–el*, *–en*, and *–er* tend to be masculine.

Onkel	uncle
Mantel	overcoat
Wagen	car
Brunnen	well, fountain
Lehrer	teacher
Keller	basement, cellar

Nouns that end in *–ung*, *–heit*, *–keit*, *–in*, and *–ie* are feminine.

Zeitung	newspaper
Gesundheit	health
Einsamkeit	loneliness
Lehrerin	(female) teacher
Industrie	industry

Many that end in *–e* are also feminine.

Lampe	lamp
Kreide	chalk
Küche	kitchen
Tante	aunt

Nouns that end in *–chen* and *–lein* are diminutives and are neuter.

Mädchen	girl
Vöglein	little bird

Sometimes a noun can have two genders. In such cases, the noun usually has two different meanings. For example, the masculine form of *See* means "lake." When it's feminine it means "sea."

Foreign Words

German is a very rich and diverse language because there is no reluctance to use foreign words. If a word in another language is especially efficient and practical, it is readily accepted as part of the German language. This is especially true of English words that describe technology or contemporary culture and trends. Although the English words are most often pronounced as they are in English, the gender is usually the same as the German word of the same meaning.

English Word Used in German	German Gender Word
der Chatroom	*der Raum* (room)
das Sandwich	*das Butterbrot* (slice of bread with butter)
die Software	*die Ware* (article, goods)

The Art of Articles

There are two kinds of articles in German: definite articles and indefinite articles. Definite articles identify a specific noun or group of nouns (the boy, the cars). Indefinite articles identify a noun or group of nouns in general (a boy, cars). German articles must agree with the noun in gender and number.

Definite Articles

The German definite article has three basic forms in the singular and one basic form in the plural, all having the meaning "the":

der	masculine/singular	*der Mann* (the man)
die	feminine/singular	*die Frau* (the woman)
das	neuter/singular	*das Kind* (the child)
die	plural	*die Kinder* (the children)

ALERT **Alert**

Don't confuse the singular feminine article *die* with the plural article *die*. When nouns become plural, their definite article is *die*, no matter what gender they were in the singular.

Indefinite Articles

The German indefinite articles correspond to the English articles "a" and "an" and are also used for the number "one." There are two forms of the German indefinite article, and, like English, the indefinite form of the plural is a plural noun standing alone without any article.

ein	masculine/singular	*ein Mann* (a man)
	neuter/singular	*ein Kind* (a child)
eine	feminine/singular	*eine Frau* (a woman)
	plural	*Kinder* (children)

The indefinite articles function in the same way with foreign words.

ein	masculine/singular	*ein Computer* (a computer)
	neuter/singular	*ein Modem* (a modem)
eine	feminine/singular	*eine Maus* (a mouse)
	plural	*Computer* (computers)

The indefinite article is also used to enumerate one of something: *Ich habe ein Buch und zwei Hefte.* (I have one book and two notebooks.) *Ich habe ein Sweatshirt und drei Bluejeans.* (I have one sweatshirt and three pairs of blue jeans.) When referring to someone's profession with verbs like *sein* (to be) and *werden* (to become), unlike English, no article is required: *Ich bin Professor.* (I am a professor.)

Declensions

When nouns are used as the subject of a sentence, they are said to be in the nominative case. The nominative definite and indefinite articles are those illustrated in the previous section. However, the articles sometimes change depending upon how a noun is used in a sentence. For example, if a masculine noun is used as a direct object in a sentence, it is in the accusative case and requires a change of the article: *Ich kenne den Mann*. (I know the man.) As direct objects, feminine, neuter, and plural articles require no changes. If a foreign word is masculine, it requires the same accusative case change when it is a direct object: *Ich kenne den DJ*. (I know the DJ.)

Certain prepositions and other functions cause other changes. These changes are described as the dative case and the genitive case. These changes of the articles are called declensions. Let's look at the declension of the definite articles.

	Masculine	**Feminine**
nominative	*der Garten*	*die Lampe*
accusative	*den Garten*	*die Lampe*
dative	*dem Garten*	*der Lampe*
genitive	*des Gartens*	*der Lampe*

	Neuter	**Plural**
nominative	*das Haus*	*die Lampen*
accusative	*das Haus*	*die Lampen*
dative	*dem Haus*	*den Lampen*
genitive	*des Hauses*	*der Lampen*

The indefinite articles follow a similar pattern.

	Masculine	**Feminine**
nominative	*ein Garten*	*eine Lampe*
accusative	*einen Garten*	*eine Lampe*
dative	*einem Garten*	*einer Lampe*
genitive	*eines Gartens*	*einer Lampe*

	Neuter	**Plural**
nominative	*ein Haus*	*Lampen*
accusative	*ein Haus*	*Lampen*
dative	*einem Haus*	*Lampen*
genitive	*eines Hauses*	*Lampen*

Foreign words used in German follow the same declensional patterns.

	Masculine	**Feminine**
nominative	*der Monitor*	*die Website*
accusative	*den Monitor*	*die Website*
dative	*dem Monitor*	*der Website*
genitive	*des Monitors*	*der Website*

	Neuter	**Plural**
nominative	*das Internet*	*die DVD-Player*
accusative	*das Internet*	*die DVD-Player*
dative	*dem Internet*	*den DVD-Player*
genitive	*des Internets*	*der DVD-Player*

Indefinite articles follow the same pattern.

Accusative Case

Articles change to their accusative case form when the noun is a direct object. Ask "whom" or "what" of the verb in a sentence to identify the direct object. For example: "They kiss the girl." Ask, "Whom do they kiss?" The answer is "the girl"—the direct object. In German, the noun that is the direct object must appear in the accusative case:

Masculine: *Sie küssen den Mann.* (They kiss the man.)
Feminine: *Sie küssen die Frau.* (They kiss the woman.)
Neuter: *Sie küssen das Mädchen.* (They kiss the girl.)
Plural: *Sie küssen die Frauen.* (They kiss the women.)

Some prepositions signal that the noun following them must be in the accusative case. These include *durch* (through), *für* (for), *gegen* (against), *ohne* (without), and *um* (around).

Masculine: *Er arbeitet für den Mann.*
(He works for the man.)
Feminine: *Er arbeitet für die Lehrerin.*
(He works for the teacher.)
Neuter: *Er arbeitet für das Mädchen.*
(He works for the girl.)
Plural: *Er arbeitet für die Schwestern.*
(He works for the sisters.)

Dative Case

The dative case is used to identify the indirect object in a sentence. The indirect object is identified by asking "to whom" or "for whom" of the verb in the sentence. For example: "I give the girl red roses." Ask, "To whom do I give red roses?" The answer is "the girl"—the indirect object. In German, the indirect object must be in the dative case:

Masculine: *Ich gebe dem Mann rote Rosen.*
(I give the man red roses.)
Feminine: *Ich gebe der Lehrerin rote Rosen.*
(I give the teacher red roses.)
Neuter: *Ich gebe dem Mädchen rote Rosen.*
(I give the girl red roses.)
Plural: *Ich gebe den Mädchen rote Rosen.*
(I give the girls red roses.)

Some prepositions are signals that the noun that follows them must be in the dative case. Some of these are *aus* (out [of]), *bei* (by, at), *mit* (with), *nach* (after), *seit* (since), *von* (from, of), and *zu* (to).

Masculine: *Ich spreche mit dem Lehrer.*
(I speak with the teacher.)
Feminine: *Ich spreche mit der Mutter.*
(I speak with the mother.)
Neuter: *Ich spreche mit dem Kind.*
(I speak with the child.)
Plural: *Ich spreche mit den Lehrerinnen.*
(I speak with the teachers.)

Genitive Case

The genitive case is used to show possession. In English, this is achieved by an apostrophe plus the letter *s* or with the preposition "of" (the man's book/the roar of a lion). In German, the genitive case replaces both forms of English possession.

Masculine: *Wo ist das Buch des Mannes?*
(Where is the man's book?)
Feminine: *Wo ist das Buch der Lehrerin?*
(Where is the teacher's book?)
Neuter: *Wo ist das Buch des Kindes?*
(Where is the child's book?)
Plural: *Wo ist das Buch der Kinder?*
(Where is the children's book?)

Some prepositions are signals that the nouns that follow them must be in the genitive case. Two of these are *während* (during) and *wegen* (because of). In a sentence, they are used like this:

Masculine: *Wo warst du während des Winters?*
(Where were you during the winter?)
Feminine: *Wo warst du während der Woche?*
(Where were you during the week?)
Neuter: *Wegen des Gewitters bleibe ich zu Hause.*
(Because of the storm I stay home.)
Plural: *Wegen der Probleme bleibe ich zu Hause.*
(Because of the problems I stay home.)

The indefinite articles function in the four cases in the same way as the definite articles. For example:

Sie küssen einen Mann. (They kiss a man.)
Wir arbeiten für eine Lehrerin. (We work for a teacher.)
Sie sprechen mit einem Kind. (They speak with a child.)
Das ist das Auto eines Lehrers. (That's a teacher's car.)

Although the use of German articles is quite different from English, you will discover with time and practice that these declensions will fall into place for you. Be patient. There is no need to absorb all these endings immediately; don't be afraid to experiment with them. And if you use the wrong case, German speakers will still understand you.

Verbs Perform the Action for You

A verb is the word that describes the action in a sentence. It can describe something that happens (I eat/we learn), movement to a place (he runs/she flies), or a state of being (they are sick/I become tired). German verbs have to be conjugated, meaning they require specific endings depending upon what subject is using them. This occurs in English, too, primarily in the present tense. For example, you say "I see" but "he sees." The third person singular in English requires an –s ending on most verbs. The verb "to be" has an even more complicated conjugation: "I am," "you are," "he is," "we are," "they are." In the other tenses, English verbs tend not to have conjugational endings. In the past tense, all the persons have the same form: "I had/he had, we spoke/ he spoke." But the verb "to be" is an exception: "I was," "you were," "he was," "we were," "they were."

German also has conjugational endings, but unlike English, these endings are required for all persons and in all tenses. The basic form of a verb is the infinitive. English infinitives begin with the particle "to," for example: "to come," "to sing," "to have," "to bring." In German, many infinitives end in –en; for example: *kommen*, *singen*, *haben, bringen.* Some infinitives end in *–n*: *sein* (to be), *tun* (to do).

In order to conjugate a German verb, you have to drop the infinitive ending (*–n* or *–en*) and add the appropriate endings. Those endings are determined by the number, person, voice, mood, and tense of the verb in a sentence. At first glance, you may feel that German conjugations are quite complicated, but you will discover that the conjugations follow very consistent patterns.

Number, Person, Subject Pronouns

In order to conjugate verbs, you need to be acquainted with the subject pronouns. Number refers to singular or plural. Person is defined as first person, second person, and third person. Therefore, subject pronouns are described as first person singular (I) and plural (we), second person singular and plural (you), and third person singular (he, she, it) and plural (they). The German subject pronouns are:

	Singular	**Plural**
1st person	*ich* (I)	*wir* (we)
2nd person	*du* (you)	*ihr* (you)/*Sie* (you)
3rd person	*er* (he, it)	*sie* (they)
	sie (she, it)	
	es (it)	

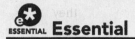

ESSENTIAL Essential

> There are three words that mean "you" in German: *du*, *ihr*, and *Sie*. The pronoun *du* is singular and informal. Use it when speaking to children, family members, and friends. Its plural form is *ihr*. The pronoun *Sie* should be used when speaking on a formal basis to one person or to a group.

The verbs *duzen* and *siezen* are used when describing the kind of relationship you have with another person: *Wir duzen einander* or *Wir duzen uns* (informal relationship: We say *du* to one another). *Wir siezen einander* or *Wir siezen uns* (formal relationship: We say *Sie* to one another).

Replacing Nouns with Pronouns

When you replace a noun with a subject pronoun, the pronoun must be of the same gender and number as the noun it replaces. But remember that even inanimate nouns can be masculine or feminine, and some animates can be neuter, especially when they are diminutives (*das Mädchen, das Vöglein*). Choose the pronoun that replaces a noun carefully; inanimate nouns are replaced by "it" in English, but not necessarily in German.

Noun	Pronoun Replacement	English Translation
der Onkel (uncle)	*er*	he
das Land (country)	*es*	it

die Kinder (children)	*sie*	they
die Häuser (houses)	*sie*	they
der Stuhl (chair)	*er*	it
die Tante (aunt)	*sie*	she
die Kreide (chalk)	*sie*	it
das Kind (child)	*es*	he/she
der Computer (computer)	*er*	it
die E-Mail (e-mail)	*sie*	it
der Laptop (laptop)	*es*	it

All plural nouns, whether animate or inanimate, are replaced by *sie* (they).

Wo ist der Stuhl? Wo ist er?
(Where is the chair? Where is it?)

Wo ist Tante Luise? Wo ist sie?
(Where is Aunt Luise? Where is she?)

Wo ist das Buch? Wo ist es?
(Where is the book? Where is it?)

Many English sentences begin with the word "it" when "it" is not the replacement of a specific noun. In that kind of usage, "it" is called an impersonal pronoun. The German pronoun *es* functions in the same way.

Es ist kalt. (It's cold.)
Es wird spät. (It's getting late.)

Endings Make the Difference

The conjugation of German verbs is a bit more complicated than the conjugation of English verbs. You'll notice that similar endings are used in all the conjugations. That's helpful; it means you can apply the same endings to new verbs as they come along. Let's look at the present tense of some frequently used verbs: *kommen*, *singen*, *sein*, and *haben*.

kommen (to come)

ich komme (I come)	*wir kommen* (we come)
du kommst (you come)	*ihr kommt* (you come)
er kommt (he comes)	*Sie kommen* (you come)
sie kommt (she comes)	*sie kommen* (they come)
es kommt (it comes)	

singen (to sing)

ich singe (I sing)	*wir singen* (we sing)
du singst (you sing)	*ihr singt* (you sing)
er singt (he sings)	*Sie singen* (you sing)
sie singt (she sings)	*sie singen* (they sing)
es singt (it sings)	

sein (to be)

ich bin (I am)	*wir sind* (we are)
du bist (you are)	*ihr seid* (you are)
er ist (he is)	*Sie sind* (you are)
sie ist (she is)	*sie sind* (they are)
es ist (it is)	

haben (to have)

ich habe (I have)	*wir haben* (we have)
du hast (you have)	*ihr habt* (you have)

er hat (he has)	*Sie haben* (you have)
sie hat (she has)	*sie haben* (they have)
es hat (it has)	

If the verb is a foreign word, it has to have the appropriate conjugational ending for each person just like other verbs.

surfen **(to surf)**

ich surfe (I surf)	*wir surfen* (we surf)
du surfst (you surf)	*ihr surft* (you surf)
er surft (he surfs)	*Sie surfen* (you surf)
sie surft (she surfs)	*sie surfen* (they surf)

There are three pronouns that are spelled alike. One is the third person singular pronoun *sie* that means "she" or "it." Since it is singular, the verb that accompanies it will have a third person singular ending: *Sie ist. Sie singt.* (She is. She sings.) Another *sie* is the third person plural pronoun that means "they." Since it is plural, the verb that accompanies it will have a third person plural ending: *Sie sind. Sie singen.* (They are. They sing.) The third *Sie* means formal "you" and is also used with a plural verb ending. It is distinguished from *sie* (they) by context. For example: *Herr Braun, sind Sie krank?* (Mr. Braun, are you sick?) *Wo sind die Mädchen? Sind sie krank?* (Where are the girls? Are they sick?) Another difference is that *Sie* (you) is always capitalized.

In Good Voice

Voice in German refers to the active voice and the passive voice. The active voice describes an action that is performed by the subject of the sentence, often on a direct object: John kisses Mary. The passive voice places the subject in a passive position in the sentence and makes the direct object the subject: Mary is kissed by John. Although some argue that using the passive voice in English is poor style, it is a high-frequency structure in German.

Getting in the Mood

Mood in German refers to the indicative mood, the imperative, and the subjunctive mood.

- The indicative mood is the most common way of making a statement. *Herr Braun ist krank.* (Mr. Braun is sick.)
- The imperative is a command. *Sprechen Sie Deutsch!* (Speak German!)
- The subjunctive mood describes a conditional idea or one that shows a cause and an effect. *Wenn er nur hier wäre.* (If only he were here.) *Wenn er hier wäre, würde ich mit ihm tanzen.* (If he were here, I'd dance with him.)

Tenses

The main tenses covered in this book are the present, past, and future tenses. They are formed much like English tenses. You have previously encountered some present tense examples with *kommen*, *singen*, *sein*, and *haben*.

The regular past tense in English ends in *–ed*. The German regular past tense ends in *–te*. For example: *Ich fragte ihn.* (I asked him.)

The German future tense is formed by the conjugation of *werden* plus an infinitive. For example: *Die Kinder werden ihn fragen.* (The children will ask him.)

Adjectives

An adjective is a word that modifies a noun or a pronoun. Just like English, German has two ways of using an adjective. Many adjectives follow a linking verb like "to be" or "to become" and are called predicate adjectives. *Frau Benz ist krank.* (Mrs. Benz is sick.) *Es wird kalt.* (It's getting cold.) Other adjectives can be placed before the noun. *Wo ist der kranke Mann?* (Where is the sick man?) Adjectives that are not predicate adjectives require endings. Adjectives of this type are:

- Possessive adjectives: *mein, meine* (my), *dein, deine* (singular informal your), *sein, seine* (his, its), *ihr, ihre* (her), *unser, unsere* (our), *euer, eure* (plural informal your), *Ihr, Ihre* (formal your), *and ihr, ihre* (their)
- Demonstrative adjectives: *dieser, diese* (this, these) and *jener, jene* (that, those)
- Interrogative adjectives: *welcher, welche* (which)

Der-words

This category of adjectives is named *der*-words because the adjective functions like the definite article, meaning that the gender of the noun is identified in the *der*-word. Some of the *der*-words are *dieser* (this), *jener* (that), and *jeder* (each). Note that *jeder* is only used in the singular. When these adjectives modify a noun, they show the gender or number of the noun by their ending.

Masculine: *der Mann, dieser Mann, jener Mann, jeder Mann* (the, this, that, each man)
Feminine: *die Frau, diese Frau, jene Frau, jede Frau* (the, this, that, each woman)
Neuter: *das Haus, dieses Haus, jenes Haus, jedes Haus* (the, this, that, each house)
Plural: *die Kinder, diese Kinder, jene Kinder* (the, these, those children)

Ein-words

This category of adjectives is named *ein*-words because the adjective functions like the indefinite article, meaning that an ending is required only for the feminine and the plural. The *ein*-words are the possessive adjectives and *kein* (no, not any).

Masculine: *ein Mann, dein Mann, ihr Mann, kein Mann* (a, your, her, no husband)
Feminine: *eine Frau, seine Frau, Ihre Frau, keine Frau* (a, his, your, no wife)
Neuter: *ein Kind, mein Kind, unser Kind, kein Kind* (a, my, our, no child)
Plural: *deine Kinder, eure Kinder, ihre Kinder, keine Kinder* (your, your, her, no children)

Adverbs

Adverbs are simpler to use than adjectives because there are no endings to consider. An adverb that describes time precedes an adverb that describes manner (by car, by bus, on foot). An adverb that describes manner precedes an adverb that describes place. Adverbs modify verbs, adjectives, and other adverbs.

Modified verb: *Sie laufen schnell.*
(They run fast.)
Modified adjective: *Mein Vater ist sehr krank.*
(My father is very sick.)
Modified adverb: *Sie sprechen zu schnell.*
(You speak too fast.)

Know Your Pronouns

You have encountered other pronouns besides subject pronouns in the nominative case. There are also accusative pronouns, dative pronouns, reflexive pronouns, and relative pronouns. The list may seem long, but all pronouns follow a simple and logical pattern.

Accusative Pronouns

The accusative case is required when a noun is a direct object or when it follows an accusative preposition (*durch, für, gegen, ohne, um*). The same is true of pronouns: They can be used as direct objects or can follow an accusative preposition. The German accusative case pronouns are:

mich (me)
dich (you [singular, informal])
ihn (him, it)
sie (her, it)
es (it)
uns (us)
euch (you [plural, informal])
Sie (you [singular/plural, formal])
sie (them)

In a sentence, the direct object pronoun follows the verb.

Sie findet es. (She finds it.)
Er liebt uns. (He loves us.)
Ich kenne dich. (I know you.)

With prepositions, the pronouns appear like this:

Er arbeitet für euch. (He works for you.)
Sie kommt ohne ihn. (She comes without him.)

Dative Pronouns

The dative case is required for indirect objects and following a dative preposition (*aus, bei, mit, nach, seit, von, zu*). In a sentence, the indirect object pronoun follows the verb. The German dative case pronouns are:

mir (me)   *dir* (you [singular, informal])
ihm (him, it)   *ihr* (her, it)
ihm (it)   *uns* (us)
euch (you [plural, informal])
Ihnen (you [singular/plural, formal])   *ihnen* (them)

In a sentence, indirect object pronouns precede the direct object if it is a noun. Indirect object pronouns follow the direct object if it is a pronoun.

Ich gebe dir das Geld. (I give you the money.)
Ich gebe es dir. (I give it to you.)

With prepositions, the pronouns appear like this:

Helga spricht mit ihnen. (Helga speaks with them.)
Sie wohnen bei ihm. (They live with him [at his house].)

Reflexive Pronouns

German reflexive pronouns can be in either the accusative case or the dative case and resemble the accusative and dative pronouns closely. Only their function is different.

Accusative	Dative	English
mich	*mir*	myself
dich	*dir*	yourself (singular, informal)
sich	*sich*	himself, itself
sich	*sich*	herself, itself
sich	*sich*	itself
uns	*uns*	ourselves
euch	*euch*	yourselves (plural, informal)
sich	*sich*	yourself, yourselves (singular, plural, formal)
sich	*sich*	themselves

The reflexive pronouns are used when the subject and the object in a sentence are the same person or thing.

Sie kauft ihm eine Jacke. (She buys him a jacket.)
Sie kauft sich eine Jacke. (She buys herself a jacket.)

Verbs that usually require a reflexive pronoun are called reflexive verbs. Some of the most common ones are:

sich anziehen	to dress oneself
sich ausziehen	to undress oneself
sich duschen	to take a shower
sich freuen	to be glad
sich hinlegen	to lie down
sich rasieren	to shave oneself
sich setzen	to seat oneself, sit down
sich waschen	to wash oneself

When a reflexive verb is conjugated, the appropriate reflexive pronoun must be used.

ich setze mich	I sit down (I seat myself)
du setzt dich	you sit down (you seat yourself)
er setzt sich	he sits down (he seats himself)
wir setzen uns	we sit down (we seat ourselves)
Sie setzen sich	you sit down (you seat yourself, yourselves)
ihr setzt sich	you sit down (you seat yourselves)
sie setzen sich	they sit down (they seat themselves)

Relative Pronouns

The German relative pronouns are *der*-words—the definite articles or *welcher*. Just like English relative pronouns, German relative pronouns link a relative clause

57

to a main clause. This occurs when the same noun is in both clauses. Two sentences such as "He knows the man. The man bought my car." become one sentence "He knows the man who bought my car." The English relative pronouns (who, whom, whose, that, which) can be replaced by either a definite article or *welcher*, which closely follow the *der*-word declensional pattern.

	Masculine	**Feminine**
nominative	*der/welcher*	*die/welche*
accusative	*den/welchen*	*die/welche*
dative	*dem/welchem*	*der/welcher*
genitive	*dessen*	*deren*

	Neuter	**Plural**
nominative	*das/welches*	*die/welche*
accusative	*das/welches*	*die/welche*
dative	*dem/welchem*	*denen/welchen*
genitive	*dessen*	*deren*

The relative pronoun that replaces a noun must be the same number, gender, and case as the noun. For example:

Wo ist der Mann, der Deutsch spricht?
(Where is the man who speaks German?)

Wo ist die Frau, die Deutsch spricht?
(Where is the woman who speaks German?)

Wo ist das Mädchen, das Deutsch spricht?
(Where is the girl who speaks German?)

Wo sind die Kinder, die Deutsch sprechen?

(Where are the children who speak German?)

If the relative pronoun in the relative clause is used as the subject, it will be in the nominative case. As a direct object or after an accusative preposition, it will be in the accusative case. As an indirect object or after a dative preposition, it will be in the dative case. The genitive case is used to show possession, where in English the relative pronoun can be "whose" or "of which."

Being Negative

Negation in German is very much like English. It can be done in two ways: by inserting the negative adverb *nicht* (not) or by using the *ein*-word *kein* as a modifier. For example:

Sie wohnt nicht in Berlin. (She doesn't live in Berlin.)
Er sendet mir keine E-Mail. (He doesn't send me an e-mail.)
Es gibt keine Milch. (There is no milk.)
Ich habe kein Geld. (I don't have any money.)

 Fact

There are other negative adverbs like *nicht*. They, too, follow the verb in a sentence. Some examples are: *niemals* (never), *noch nicht* (not yet), and *nicht mehr* (no more). Two negatives are the pronouns *niemand* and *nichts*: *Niemand wohnt hier.* (No one lives here.) *Ich verstehe nichts.* (I don't understand anything.)

Asking Questions

Just like English, German has more than one way to ask a question. Sometimes just intoning your voice while you make a statement is a question. Other questions require a yes or no answer. Still others begin with an interrogative word.

Yes or No Questions

When asking a question that can be answered by either *ja* (yes) or *nein* (no), invert the subject and the verb to make a question.

Statement: *Er kommt um acht Uhr.*
(He's coming at eight o'clock.)

Question: *Kommt er um acht Uhr?*
(Is he coming at eight o'clock?)

Statement: *Deine Schwester singt gut.*
(Your sister sings well.)

Question: *Singt deine Schwester gut?*
(Does your sister sing well?)

Using Interrogative Words

Interrogative words ask questions about specific elements in a sentence: "how," "when," "where," "why," "who," "what."

Common Interrogative Words

wer	who
was	what
wann	when
wo	where
wie	how
warum	why

A question that begins with an interrogative word requires the inversion of the subject and verb, just like in a yes-no question.

Statement: *Du hast kein Geld.*
(You don't have any money.)

Question: *Warum hast du kein Geld?*
(Why don't you have any money?)

Statement: *Er findet eine Zeitung.*
(He finds a newspaper.)

Question: *Was findet er?*
(What does he find?)

Statement: *Sie kommen um acht Uhr.*
(They're coming at eight o'clock.)

Question: *Wann kommen sie?*
(When are they coming?)

Chapter 3

Essential German

This chapter provides you with some of the most essential German vocabulary for travelers. It includes practical phrases like "Do you speak English?" and "I don't understand" as well as polite phrases, yes and no, numbers, calendar vocabulary, and instructions for telling time.

Survival German

The following German phrases just might come in handy as you make your way into the German-speaking world. Refer to Chapter 1 and the Pronunciation Key. In the phonetics, the capitalized syllable is the stressed syllable.

I speak a little German.
Ich spreche ein bisschen Deutsch.
eech SHPRECH eh ine BISS chen doitch

Do you speak English?
Sprechen Sie Englisch?
SHPREHCH en zee ENG lish

What does that mean?
Was bedeutet das?
vuss beh DOIT et duss

How do you say . . . in German?
Wie sagt man . . . auf Deutsch?
vee zahkt munn . . . owf doitch

Repeat, please.
Wiederholen Sie, bitte.
vee duh HOLE en zee BIT teh

More slowly. One more time.
Langsamer. Noch einmal.
LUNG zah muh noch ine MUHL

I don't understand.
Ich verstehe nicht.
eech fair SHTAY eh nicht

I don't know. What?
Ich weiß nicht. Wie bitte?
eech VICE nicht VEE bit teh

ESSENTIAL Essential

Don't be afraid to use the German you know and to experiment. Germans understand that foreigners can make errors in their language, but appreciate the effort when someone uses German. Besides, it's good practice and will give you the confidence to speak and be heard.

Language Basics

The following vocabulary is quite basic but very useful.

Language Basics

yes	*ja*	yah
no	*nein*	nine
OK	*OK*	OK
and	*und*	oont
or	*oder*	OH duh
but	*aber*	AH buh
who	*wer*	vare
what	*was*	vuss
when	*wann*	vunn
where	*wo*	voe

where (to)	*wohin*	voe HIN
why	*warum*	vah ROOM
how	*wie*	vee

Being Polite

It's just common sense to be polite when you're a guest in a country. Saying "please" and "thank you" are the essentials for being a good guest.

Polite Vocabulary

please	*bitte*
	BIT teh
thanks	*danke*
	DUNN keh
thank you	*danke schön*
	DUNK eh shern
thank you so much	*vielen Dank*
	FEEL en dunk
thank you very much	*danke sehr*
	DUNN keh zare
you're welcome	*bitte schön*
	BIT teh shern
it was my pleasure	*gern geschehen*
	gairn gheh SHAY en
don't mention it	*keine Ursache*
	KINE eh OOR zuch eh
pardon me	*Verzeihen Sie*
	fare TSY en zee
excuse me	*Entschuldigung*
	ent SHOOL dee goong

I'm sorry	*es tut mir Leid*	
	ess TOOT meer LITE	
bless you	*Gesundheit*	
(after a sneeze)	gheh ZOONT hite	
cheers	*prost*	
	prohst	

 Alert

Use *Verzeihen Sie* to mean "excuse me" or "pardon me" in the sense that you are looking to be forgiven for an action. *Entschuldigung* is more of an apology and is used when asking for someone's attention.

Titles

| Mr. | *Herr* | hare |
| Mrs., Ms. | *Frau* | frow |

Please don't let me disturb you.
Bitte lassen Sie sich nicht stören.
BIT teh LUSS en zee zeech nicht SHTER en

Enjoy your meal!
Guten Appetit!
GOOT en ah peh TEET

Please click on this link.
Klicken Sie bitte auf diesen Link.
KLICK en zee ouf DEE zen link

It's Time to Count

Do you remember the line from a children's rhyme that says "four and twenty blackbirds baked in a pie?" That will come in handy as you learn to use the German numbers between twenty and a hundred.

Numbers

one	*eins*	ince
two	*zwei*	tsvy
three	*drei*	dry
four	*vier*	fear
five	*fünf*	fuenf
six	*sechs*	zex
seven	*sieben*	ZEE ben
eight	*acht*	ahcht
nine	*neun*	noin
ten	*zehn*	tsayn
eleven	*elf*	elf
twelve	*zwölf*	tsverlf
thirteen	*dreizehn*	DRY tsayn
fourteen	*vierzehn*	FEAR tsayn
fifteen	*fünfzehn*	FUENF tsayn
sixteen	*sechzehn*	ZEX tsayn
seventeen	*siebzehn*	ZEEP tsayn
eighteen	*achtzehn*	AHCHT tsayn
nineteen	*neunzehn*	NOIN tsayn
twenty	*zwanzig*	TSVUNN tsik
twenty-one	*einundzwanzig*	ine oont TSVUNN tsik
twenty-two	*zweiundzwanzig*	tsvy oont TSVUNN tsik
twenty-three	*dreiundzwanzig*	dry oont TSVUNN tsik

From twenty to a hundred, the number in the second position is said before the number in the first position (twenty-four): "four and twenty blackbirds," *vierundzwanzig Amseln*. The first number to do this is twenty-one; the last is ninety-nine.

Numbers 30 and Up

thirty	*dreißig*	DRY sik
forty	*vierzig*	FEAR tsik
fifty	*fünfzig*	FUENF tsik
sixty	*sechzig*	ZEX tsik
seventy	*siebzig*	ZEEP tsik
eighty	*achtzig*	AHCHT tsik
ninety	*neunzig*	NOIN tsik
100	*hundert*	HOON dairt
200	*zweihundert*	TSVY hoon dairt
1,000	*tausend*	TOW zent
3,000	*dreitausend*	DRY tow zent
1,000,000	*eine Million*	ine eh MEEL ee own
2,000,000	*zwei Millionen*	tsvy MEEL ee own en
1 billion	*eine Milliarde*	ine eh MEEL ee ahr deh
1 trillion	*eine Billion*	ine eh BEEL ee own

Take care not to confuse the German *Billion* (trillion) with the English "billion." When German numbers get long, they become compounds of the numbers involved: *fünfunddreißigtausendsiebenhundertzweiundfünfzig*. That is, they are written as one word. Therefore, it is most common to show the compound number as a numeral. Unlike English, every three German digits are separated by a decimal: 350.752.

What Time Is It?

German does not use A.M. or P.M. to designate time between midnight and noon and between noon and midnight. Instead, the twenty-four-hour or military clock is used. That means that 2 A.M. is said as *zwei Uhr*, but 2 P.M. is said as *vierzehn Uhr*.

What time is it? It's . . .
Wie viel Uhr ist es? Es ist . . .
vee feel OOR ist ess; ess ist

one o'clock	*ein Uhr*
	ine OOR
two o'clock	*zwei Uhr*
	tsvy OOR
3:30	*halb vier*
	hulp FEAR
4:15	*Viertel nach vier/vier Uhr fünfzehn*
	FEAR tel nahch fear/fear OOR FUENF tsayn
4:45	*Viertel vor fünf/vier Uhr fünfundvierzig*
	FEAR tel for FUENF/fear OOR fuenf oont
	FEAR tsik
5:10	*zehn (Minuten) nach fünf*
	tsayn (mee NOO ten) nahch FUENF
6:50	*zehn (Minuten) vor sechs*
	tsayn (mee NOO ten) for ZEX
7 A.M.	*sieben Uhr*
	zee ben OOR
3 P.M.	*fünfzehn Uhr*
	fuenf tsayn OOR
6 P.M.	*achtzehn Uhr*
	ahcht tsayn OOR

noon	*Mittag*
	MIT tahk
midnight	*Mitternacht*
	MIT air nahcht

Fact

When stating a time in the P.M. hours, the designations of *Viertel* (quarter) and *halb* (half) cannot be used, and the hour is stated followed by the number of minutes. For example: *siebzehn Uhr zwanzig* (5:20 P.M.), *zwanzig Uhr dreißig* (8:30 P.M.), and *zweiundzwanzig Uhr fünfundvierzig* (10:45 P.M.).

The Calendar

The German calendar starts on Monday and is otherwise set up like the calendar that English speakers use.

Days of the Week

Monday	*Montag*	MONE tahk
Tuesday	*Dienstag*	DEENS tahk
Wednesday	*Mittwoch*	MIT vawch
Thursday	*Donnerstag*	DAWN airs tahk
Friday	*Freitag*	FRY tahk
Saturday	*Samstag/Sonnabend*	ZAHMS tahk/
		ZAWN ah bent
Sunday	*Sonntag*	ZAWN tahk

Months of the Year

January	*Januar*	YAH noo ar
February	*Februar*	FAY broo ar
March	*März*	MAIRTS
April	*April*	ah PRILL
May	*Mai*	my
June	*Juni*	YOO nee
July	*Juli*	YOO lee
August	*August*	ow GOOST
September	*September*	zep TEM buh
October	*Oktober*	awk TOE buh
November	*November*	no VEM buh
December	*Dezember*	day TSEM buh

Chapter 4

Meeting People

As you travel through the German-speaking world, it will be important to know how to greet people and exchange pleasantries in the local language. Not only will this make your travels a lot easier, but it will also give you a greater insight into how people in other countries interact. The traveler who knows nothing about the local language misses out on so much. So, say hello and have a friendly chat with your hosts. It will make your journey that much more enjoyable.

Greetings

It is common courtesy in Germany to say hello to the clerk when you enter a shop or store. When you're finished browsing or shopping, it's customary to say goodbye.

Saying Hello

hello, hi	*hallo*	hAH low
good morning	*guten Morgen*	gOO ten MORE gen
good day, hello	*guten Tag*	gOO ten tahk
good evening	*guten Abend*	gOO ten AH bent

Leave-Takings

bye, so long	*tschüss*	chuess
goodbye	*auf Wiedersehen*	owf VEE duh zane
good night	*gute Nacht*	GOO teh nahcht
see you later	*bis später*	biss SHPAY tuh
see you in a while	*bis gleich*	biss glych
see you tomorrow	*bis morgen*	biss MORE gen
goodbye (telephone)	*auf Wiederhören*	owf VEE duh hern

When you ask "How are you?" you must take into consideration what kind of relationship you have with the person you are speaking to, formal or informal. In general, you can say:

Wie geht's?   vee gates

Another informal version that you would use with people to whom you say *du* is:

Wie geht es dir?   vee gate ess deer

The plural informal (*ihr*) question is:

Wie geht es euch?   vee gate ess oich

And the formal singular or plural (*Sie*) question is:

Wie geht es Ihnen? vee gate ess EE nen

Appropriate Responses

fine, well	*gut*	goot
I'm doing well.	*Es geht mir gut.*	ess gate meer goot
not well	*nicht gut*	nihct goot
not bad	*nicht schlecht*	nihct shlecht
rather well	*ziemlich gut*	TSEEM lich goot
very well	*sehr gut*	ZARE goot
I'm not doing well.	*Es geht mir*	ess gate meer
	nicht gut.	nihct goot

Introductions

When meeting people for the first time, you must still be aware of the formal or informal relationship involved. This will determine the form of your questions and answers. When asking for or giving a name, there are two basic approaches for both the formal and informal.

What's your name? (formal)
Wie heißen Sie?
vee HY sen zee

What's your name? (informal)
Wie heißt du?
vee hysst doo

What is your last name? (formal)
Wie heißen Sie mit Nachnamen?
vee HY sen zee mit NAHCH nah men

What is your last name? (informal)
Wie heißt du mit Nachnamen?
vee hysst doo mit NAHCH nah men

Her name is . . .
Sie heißt . . .
zee hysst
Ihr Name ist . . .
ear NAH meh ist

His name is . . .
Er heißt . . .
air hysst
Sein Name ist . . .
zine NAH meh ist

My name is . . .
Ich heiße . . .
eech HY seh
Mein Name ist . . .
mine NAH meh ist

Pleased to meet you. (formal)
Es freut mich Sie kennen zu lernen.
ess froit meech zee KEN en tsoo LARE nen

I'd like to introduce . . .
Ich möchte . . . vorstellen.
eech MERCH teh FOR shtell len

Alert

> When asking for or giving a name, the verb *heißen* is commonly used. Its meaning is "to be called." Therefore, you are really asking, "How are you called?" *Wie heißen Sie? Ich heiße Thomas Keller.* "My name is (I am called) Thomas Keller."

The Verb *Haben*

Haben means "to have." It is a very useful, high-frequency verb. Besides being able to stand alone in a sentence, *haben* also acts as the auxiliary of other verbs. Let's look at some sentences with this important verb.

I have a problem.
Ich habe ein Problem.
eech HAH beh ine pro BLAME

He has two computers.
Er hat zwei Computer.
air haht tsvy kom PYOO tuh

Do you have a sister? (informal)
Hast du eine Schwester?
hahst doo ine eh SHVES tuh

Do you have your passport? (formal)
Haben Sie Ihren Pass?
HAH ben zee EAR en puss

76

The verb *haben* is often used in special expressions and idioms, in which the translation is not always "to have."

I'm hungry.
Ich habe Hunger.
eech HAH beh HOONG uh

I'm thirsty.
Ich habe Durst.
eech HAH beh doorst

She's homesick.
Sie hat Heimweh.
zee haht HIME vay

Is something the matter?
Hast du was?
hahst doo vuss

He's busy.
Er hat zu tun.
air haht tsoo toon

He's fed up with that.
Er hat das satt.
air haht duss zutt

Haben in Other Tenses

The verb *haben* is just as useful in the past and future tenses as in the present tense. Let's look at its conjugation.

Present/Past/Future

ich	*habe* [HAH be]
	hatte [HAH teh]
	werde haben [VARE deh HAH ben]
du	*hast* [hahst]
	hattest [HAH test]
	wirst haben [virst HAH ben]
er/sie/es	*hat* [haht]
	hatte [HAH teh]
	wird haben [virt HAH ben]
wir	*haben* [HAH ben]
	hatten [HAH ten]
	werden haben [VARE den HAH ben]
ihr	*habt* [hahbt]
	hattet [HAH tet]
	werdet haben [VARE det HAH ben]
Sie	*haben* [HAH ben]
	hatten [HAH ten]
	werden haben [VARE den HAH ben]
sie	*haben* [HAH ben]
	hatten [HAH ten]
	werden haben [VARE den HAH ben]

If the verb is of foreign origin, it follows the same tense patterns.

ich	*surfe* [ZOOR feh]
ich	*surfte* [ZOORF teh]
ich	*habe gesurft* [HAH beh geh ZOORFT]
ich	*werde surfen* [VAIR deh ZOOR fen]

78

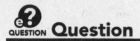

Question

> **In the future tense, do I have to place the verb that follows *werden* at the end of the sentence?**
> This is one of the areas where English and German are different. In the English future tense, the verb stands directly behind "will" or "shall." In the German future tense, the verb is the last element in the sentence. *Sie wird mit Frau Schneider sprechen.* (zee virt mit frow SHNY duh SHPREHCH en) "She will speak with Ms. Schneider."

Nationalities and Languages

As you travel, you encounter many people from many different lands. It is only natural that you talk about where you come from or that you ask about someone else's country. The following list contains the nouns that describe nationality. The masculine form is given first and is followed by *–in* to indicate the feminine form (*der Amerikaner/die Amerikanerin*). Where the feminine is formed differently, the noun is written out completely.

	Masculine	**Feminine**
African	*Afrikaner*	*–in*
	ah free KAHN uh	in
American	*Amerikaner*	*–in*
	ah mare ee KAH nuh	in
Asian	*Asiat*	*–in*
	AH zee aht	in

Austrian	*Österreicher*	*–in*
	ER stuh ryech uh	in
Belgian	*Belgier*	*–in*
	BELL ghee uh	in
Brazilian	*Brasilianer*	*–in*
	brah zee lee AH nuh	in
Canadian	*Kanadier*	*–in*
	kah nah DEE uh	in
Chinese	*Chinese*	*Chinesin*
	chee NAY zeh	chee NAY zin
Dutch	*Niederländer*	*–in*
	NEE duh lend uh	in
Egyptian	*Ägypter*	*–in*
	ay GUEP tuh	in
English	*Engländer*	*–in*
	ENG lend uh	in
European	*Europäer*	*–in*
	oy roe PAY uh	in
French	*Franzose*	*Französin*
	frahn TSOE zeh	frahn TSER zin
German	*Deutsche*	*Deutsche*
	DOITCH eh	DOITCH eh
(East) Indian	*Inder*	*–in*
	IN duh	in
Italian	*Italiener*	*–in*
	ee tah lee AY nuh	in
Japanese	*Japaner*	*–in*
	yah PAH nuh	in
Mexican	*Mexikaner*	*–in*
	mex ee KAHN uh	in

Pole	*Pole*	*Polin*
	POE leh	POE lin
Russian	*Russe*	*Russin*
	ROOS eh	ROOS in
Spaniard	*Spanier*	*–in*
	SHPAH nee uh	in
Swede	*Schwede*	*Schwedin*
	SHVAY deh	SHVAY din
Swiss	*Schweizer*	*–in*
	SHVITSE uh	in

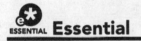 **Essential**

When using words of nationality in context, you do not have to use an indefinite article (*a, an/ein, eine*), as you do in English. "Are you an American?" *Sind Sie Amerikaner?* (zint zee ah mare ee KAH nuh); "No, I'm a Canadian." *Nein, ich bin Kanadier.* (nine eech bin kah NAH dee uh).

The Verb *Sein*

The verb *sein* (to be) is another important high-frequency verb that can stand alone in a sentence or be used as the auxiliary of other verbs. It is used with nouns, pronouns, adjectives, and a variety of adverbial expressions.

I am a German teacher.
Ich bin Lehrer für Deutsch.
eech bin LAY ruh fuer doitch

Are you sick?
Bist du krank?
bist doo krahnk

She is very pretty.
Sie ist sehr schön.
zee ist zare shern

Where are they?
Wo sind sie?
voe zint zee

They're at home.
Sie sind zu Hause.
zee zint tsoo HOW zeh

She's in Munich.
Sie ist in München.
zee ist in MUEN chen

He's over there.
Er ist dort drüben.
air ist dort DRUE ben

Sein in Other Tenses

The verb *sein* is just as useful in the past and future tenses as in the present tense. Let's look at its conjugation.

	Present/Past/Future
ich	*bin* [bin]
	war [vahr]

	werde sein [VARE deh zine]
du	*bist* [bist]
	warst [wahrst]
	wirst sein [virst zine]
er/sie/es	*ist* [ist]
	war [vahr]
	wird sein [virt zine]
wir	sind [zint]
	waren [VAHR en]
	werden sein [VARE den zine]
ihr	*seid* [zite]
	wart [vahrt]
	werdet sein [VARE det zine]
Sie	*sind* [zint]
	waren [VAHR en]
	werden sein [VARE den zine]
sie	*sind* [zint]
	waren [VAHR en]
	werden sein [VARE den zine]

The verb *sein* is used in many practical expressions. For example:

What is your occupation?
Was sind Sie von Beruf?
vuss zint zee fone beh ROOF

How is the weather?
Wie ist das Wetter?
vee ist duss VETT uh

It's cold.
Es ist kalt.
ess ist kullt

She comes from Hamburg.
Sie ist aus Hamburg.
zee ist ows HAHM boork

Is that really necessary?
Muss das sein?
moos duss zine

What can I get you? (in a store)
Was darf es sein?
vuss darf ess zine

Family Members

Talking about family is another interesting way to share information about yourself while getting to know other people.

Family Vocabulary

aunt	*eine Tante*
	ine eh TAHN tuh
brother	*ein Bruder*
	ine BROO duh
cousin (male)	*ein Cousin*
	ine koo ZAN
cousin (female)	*eine Cousine*
	ine eh koo ZEE neh
daughter	*eine Tochter*
	ine eh TAWCH tuh

father	*ein Vater*
	ine FAH tuh
granddaughter	*eine Enkelin*
	ine eh ENK ell in
grandfather	*ein Großvater*
	ine GROSS fah tuh
grandmother	*eine Großmutter*
	ine eh GROSS moo tuh
grandson (grandchild)	*ein Enkel*
	ine ENK ell
husband	*ein Mann*
	ine munn
mother	*eine Mutter*
	ine eh MOO tuh
nephew	*ein Neffe*
	ine NEFF eh
niece	*eine Nichte*
	ine eh NICH teh
siblings	*Geschwister*
	gheh SHVISS tuh
sister	*eine Schwester*
	ine eh SHVES tuh
son	*ein Sohn*
	ine zone
uncle	*ein Onkel*
	ine AWN kell
wife	*eine Frau*
	INE eh frow

Chapter 5

Airports and Hotels

Now that you know how to greet people and chat about the basics, it's time to board a plane and head for your destination. This chapter deals with the situations you might encounter at an airport or when checking into a hotel. The vocabulary will guide you in making reservations, buying tickets, boarding the plane, going through customs, and getting to your hotel.

Using *Ich Möchte*

Germans prefer to use a special verb form in place of "want." *Ich möchte* means "I would like" and is considered the polite way of requesting something.

What would you like?
Was möchten Sie?
vuss MERCH ten zee

I would like to buy an airline ticket.
Ich möchte ein Flugticket kaufen.
eech MERCH teh ine FLOOK ticket KOW fen

Many useful phrases can follow *Ich möchte* . . .

. . . to cash these traveler's checks.
. . . *diese Reiseschecks einlösen.*
DEE zeh RYE zeh shecks INE ler zen

. . . to change this into euros.
. . . *dies in Euro wechseln.*
Dees in OY roe VEX eln

. . . a train schedule.
. . . *einen Zugfahrplan.*
INE en TSOOK far plahn

. . . a room.
. . . *ein Zimmer.*
ine TSIMM uh

The conjugation of this verb in the present tense, all persons is:

ich möchte [MERCH teh]

du möchtest [MERCH test]
er, sie, es möchte [MERCH teh]
wir möchten [MERCH ten]
ihr möchtet [MERCH tet]
Sie möchten [MERCH ten]
sie möchten [MERCH ten]

The verb *wollen* (to want) is an acceptable alternative but is not as polite. In the present and past tenses, it is conjugated like this:

	Present/Past
ich	*will* [vill]
	wollte [VAWL teh]
du	*willst* [villst]
	wolltest [VAWL test]
er, sie, es	*will* [vill]
	wollte [VAWL teh]
wir	*wollen* [VAW len]
	wollten [VAWL ten]
ihr	*wollt* [vawlt]
	wolltet [VAWL tet]
Sie	*wollen* [VAW len]
	wollten [VAWL ten]
sie	*wollen* [VAW len]
	wollten [VAWL ten]

Verbs That Move You

Some verbs are called "verbs of motion" because they are used to describe getting from one place to another.

The Verb *Gehen*

The verb *gehen* means "to go," especially on foot. It is used when you are going short distances that can be reached by walking. Its present and past conjugations are:

	Present/Past
ich	*gehe* [GAY eh]
	ging [ging]
du	*gehst* [gayst]
	gingst [gingst]
er, sie, es	*geht* [gayt]
	ging [ging]
wir	*gehen* [GAY en]
	gingen [GING en]
ihr	*geht* [gayt]
	gingt [gingt]
Sie	*gehen* [GAY en]
	gingen [GING en]
sie	*gehen* [GAY en]
	gingen [GING en]

Where are you going?
Wohin gehen Sie?
voe HIN GAY en zee

I'm going home.
Ich gehe nach Hause.
eech GAY eh nahch HOW zeh

We're going to the hotel.
Wir gehen zum Hotel.
veer GAY en tsoom HOE tel

89

The Verb *Fahren*

The verb *fahren* means "to go" or "to drive" and is used to describe getting someplace by vehicle. Its present and past conjugations are:

	Present/Past
ich	*fahre* [FAHR eh]
	fuhr [foor]
du	*fährst* [fairst]
	fuhrst [foorst]
er, sie, es	*fährt* [fairt]
	fuhr [foor]
wir	*fahren* [FAHR en]
	fuhren [FOOR en]
ihr	*fahrt* [fahrt]
	fuhrt [foort]
Sie	*fahren* [FAHR en]
	fuhren [FOOR en]
sie	*fahren* [FAHR en]
	fuhren [FOOR en]

Where are they going?
Wohin fahren sie?
voe HIN FAHR en zee

They're going to the city.
Sie fahren in die Stadt.
zee FAHR en in dee SHTUTT

Are you going by bus or by train?
Fahren Sie mit dem Bus oder mit dem Zug?
FAHR en zee mitt dame boos OH duh mitt dame tsook

My husband drives very well.
Mein Mann fährt sehr gut.
mine munn fairt zare goot

 Fact

> Use the verb *fahren* to say that you are riding on or operating a vehicle: *Ich fahre ein Moped.* (I'm riding a moped.) *Er fährt ein Motorboot.* (He's driving a motorboat.)

The Verb *Fliegen*

The verb *fliegen* means "to fly." Its present and past tense conjugations are:

	Present/Past
ich	*fliege* [FLEEG eh]
	flog [flohk]
du	*fliegst* [fleegst]
	flogst [flohkst]
er, sie, es	*fliegt* [fleekt]
	flog [flohk]
wir	*fliegen* [FLEEG en]
	flogen [FLOHG en]
ihr	*fliegt* [fleekt]
	flogt [flohkt]
Sie	*fliegen* [FLEEG en]
	flogen [FLOHG en]

91

| *sie* | *fliegen* [FLEEG en] |
| | *flogen* [FLOHG en] |

Are you flying to Rome?
Fliegt ihr nach Rom?
fleekt ear nahch rome

No, we're flying to Munich.
Nein, wir fliegen nach München.
nine veer FLEEG en nahch MUEN chen

A lot of birds are flying over the lake.
Viele Vögel fliegen über dem See.
FEE leh FER ghell FLEEG en UE buh dame zay

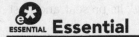
Essential

Unlike English, German is specific about how you get to a place: on foot, in a vehicle, or in a plane. So use *gehen*, *fahren*, and *fliegen* to give the appropriate meaning you want. If you asked someone in German whether he's going to Japan, you wouldn't use the verb *gehen*—"going on foot." You'd use *fliegen*—"to fly."

Airport and Flight Vocabulary

Now that you're equipped with some essential verbs, you're ready to take a trip to Germany. You can make reservations, buy your ticket, and get on a plane. Here are some German phrases that will come in handy.

People, Places, and Things

airplane	*das Flugzeug*
	duss FLOOK tsoik
airport	*der Flughafen*
	dair FLOOK hah fen
arrivals	*Ankünfte*
	AHN kuenf teh
baggage, luggage	*das Gepäck*
	duss gheh PECK
boarding pass	*die Bordkarte, Einsteigekarte*
	dee BOHRT kahr teh,
	AYN schteeg kahr teh
carry-on luggage	*das Handgepäck*
	duss HAHNT gheh peck
checked luggage	*das abgefertigte Gepäck*
	duss AHP gheh fair tick teh gheh PECK
check-in counter	*der Abfertigungsschalter*
	dair AHP fair tee goongs shull tuh
departures	*Abflüge*
	AHP flue gheh
duty-free shop	*der Duty-free-Shop*
	dair doo tee FREE shawp
early	*früh*
	frueh
identification	*der Ausweis*
	dair OWS vice
late	*spät*
	shpate
passenger	*der Fluggast/Passagier*
	dair FLOOK gust/pah sah ZHEER

passport	*der Pass*
	dair puss
pilot	*der Pilot/die –in*
	dair pee LOTE/dee in
security check	*die Sicherheitskontrolle*
	dee ZICH uh hites kawn traw leh
shuttle	*der Pendelbus*
	dair PENN dell boos
steward(ess)	*der Steward/die Stewardess*
	dair STOO art/dee STOO ahr dess
visa	*das Visum*
	duss VEE zoom

Ticket Information

airline	*die Fluggesellschaft*
	dee FLOOK gheh zell shuft
economy (coach)	*die zweite Klasse*
	dee TSVY teh KLUSS eh
first class	*die erste Klasse*
	dee AIR steh KLUSS eh
flight	*der Flug*
	dair flook
gate	*der Flugsteig*
	dair FLOOK shtike
one-way ticket	*das einfache Flugticket*
	duss INE fahch eh FLOOK ticket
plane ticket	*das Flugticket*
	duss FLOOK ticket
round-trip ticket	*die Hin- und Rückflugkarte*
	dee hin oont RUEK flook-kahr teh

stopover	*die Zwischenlandung*
	dee TSVISH en lun doong
terminal	*der Terminal*
	dair tare mee NAHL

Travel Verbs

to board	*an Bord des Flugzeugs gehen, ins Flugzeug einsteigen*
	ahn bohrt dess FLOOK tsoiks GAH en, ins FLOOK tsoik INE shty ghen
to buy a ticket	*ein Flugticket kaufen*
	ine FLOOK ticket KOW fen
to check bags	*das Gepäck aufgeben*
	duss gheh PECK OWF gay ben
to land	*landen*
	LUHN den
to reserve	*eine Reservierung machen*
	ine eh ray zare VEER oong MACH en
to sit down	*sich hinsetzen*
	zeech HIN zetz en
to take off	*starten*
	SHTAHR ten

Baggage Claim, Immigration, and Customs

When you arrive at your destination, you will need to get your luggage and go through immigration and customs. You'll find this vocabulary helpful.

Arrival and Baggage

to land	*landen*
	LUN den
arrivals	*Ankünfte*
	AHN kuenf teh
baggage claim	*die Gepäckausgabe*
	dee gheh PECK ows gah beh
My luggage is missing.	*Mein Gepäck ist verloren gegangen.*
	mine gheh PECK ist fare LORE en gheh GAHNG en

Immigration and Customs

passport control	*die Passkontrolle*
	dee PUSS kawn trawl eh
immigration form	*das Einreiseformular*
	duss INE rye zeh for moo lahr
last name, surname	*der Nachname, Familienname*
	dair NAHCH nah meh, fah MEE lee en nah meh
first name	*der Vorname*
	dair FORE nah meh
customs	*der Zoll/die Zollkontrolle*
	dair tsawl/dee tsawl kawn TRAWL eh
nothing to declare	*nichts zu erklären*
	nichts tsoo air KLARE en
customs form	*die Zollerklärung*
	dee TSAWL air klare oong
Here's my passport.	*Hier ist mein Pass.*
	heer ist mine puss
I have a visa.	*Ich habe ein Visum.*
	eech HAH beh ine VEE zoom

I don't have a visa.	*Ich habe kein Visum.*
	eech HAH beh kine VEE zoom
I would like to declare…	*Ich möchte …verzollen.*
	eech MERCH teh fare TSAWL en

At the Hotel

You've arrived! Now you need a place to clean up, rest, and unpack your things. The following words and phrases will be helpful for getting the accommodations you want.

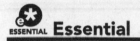

Essential

In some German hotels you have to specify what kind of room you want and with what kind of facilities. Rooms don't always come with a toilet, sink, and tub. In less-expensive hotels you will share the bathroom down the hall with other guests.

Helpful Phrases and Vocabulary

I would like a room for . . .
Ich möchte ein Zimmer für . . .
eech MERCH teh ine TSIMM uh fuer

Ich möchte ein Zimmer für . . .

one night	*eine Nacht*
	INE eh nahcht
two nights	*zwei Nächte*
	tsvy NEHCH teh

97

one person	*eine Person*
	INE eh pair ZONE
two people	*zwei Personen*
	tsvy pair ZONE en

I would like a room with . . .
Ich möchte ein Zimmer mit . . .
eech MERCH teh ine TSIMM uh mit

Ich möchte ein Zimmer mit . . .

two beds	*zwei Betten*
	tsvy BET en
a double bed	*einem Doppelbett*
	INE em DAW pell bet
a shower	*einer Dusche*
	INE ehr DOO sheh
a bathtub	*einer Badewanne*
	INE ehr BAH deh vunn eh
a toilet	*einer Toilette*
	INE ehr toy LET eh
a television	*einem Fernsehen*
	INE em fairn zay en
a telephone	*einem Telefon*
	INE em tay lay FONE
air conditioning	einer *Klimaanlage*
	INE ehr KLEE mah ahn lah gheh
Wi-Fi	WLAN
	VAY luhn

Do you have . . . ? Is there . . . ?
Haben Sie . . . ? Gibt es . . . ?
HAH ben zee, geept ess

Haben Sie . . ./Gibt es . . .

an elevator	*einen Fahrstuhl*
	INE en FAHR shtool
laundry service	*einen Wäschedienst*
	INE en VESH eh deenst
a hairdresser/barber	*einen Damenfriseur/Herrenfriseur*
	INE en DAHM en free zeur/HARE
	en free zeur
a parking lot/garage	*einen Parkplatz/eine Garage*
	INE en PARK plutz/INE eh gah
	RAH zheh
a restaurant	*ein Restaurant*
	ine ress taw RAWNG
a pool	*ein Schwimmbad*
	ine SHVIMM baht
an e-mail address	*eine E-Mail-Adresse*
	ine eh ee mail ah DRESS eh

Naturally the word *Hotel* on a sign tells you where you are. But other words identify places for lodging as well:

motel	*das Motel* [duss moe TELL]
hotel room with breakfast	*das Hotel garni* [duss hoe TELL GAHR nee]
inn	*der Gasthof* [dare GAHST hofe]
boarding house	*die Pension* [dee pahng zee OWN]

| bed and breakfast | *Zimmer frei* [TSIMM uh fry] |
| no vacancy | *belegt* [bay LAYKT] |

About Your Stay

Now that you found lodging, you need some vocabulary for getting around the hotel, paying your bill, and requesting a wake-up call.

Hotel Vocabulary

hotel	*das Hotel*
	duss HOE tell
accommodations	*die Unterkunft*
	dee OON tuh koonft
first floor (U.S.),	*das Erdgeschoss*
ground floor (UK)	duss AIRT gheh shawss
second floor (U.S.),	*die erste Etage*
first floor (UK)	dee AIR steh eh TAH zheh
hallway	*der Korridor, Flur*
	dare koe ree DORE, floor
room	*das Zimmer*
	duss TSIMM uh
door	*die Tür*
	dee tuer
window	*das Fenster*
	duss FEN stuh
bed	*das Bett*
	duss bett
pillow	*das Kissen*
	duss KISS en

sofa	*das Sofa*
	duss ZOE fuh
wardrobe	*der Kleiderschrank*
	dare KLY duh shrunk
lamp	*die Lampe*
	dee LUMP eh
bathroom	*das Badezimmer*
	duss BAH deh tsimm uh
lavatory	*die Toilette*
	dee toy LET eh
towel	*das Handtuch*
	duss HAHNT tooch

Where is . . . ?
Wo ist . . . ?
voe ist

Wo ist . . .

the elevator	*der Fahrstuhl*
	dare FAHR shtool
the laundry service	*der Wäschedienst*
	dare VESH eh deenst
the hairdresser/barber	*der Damenfriseur/Herrenfriseur*
	dare DAHM en free zeur/HARE en free zeur
the parking lot/garage	*der Parkplatz/eine Garage*
	dare PARK plutz/INE eh gah RAH zheh
the restaurant	*das Restaurant*
	duss ress taw RAWNG

the pool	*das Schwimmbad*
	duss SHVIMM baht
the reception desk	*die Rezeption*
	dee ray TSEP tsee own

I would like a wake-up call at 8 A.M.
Ich möchte um acht Uhr einen Weckanruf.
eech MERCH teh oom ahcht oor INE en VECK ahn roof

What is checkout time?
Um wie viel Uhr muss man abreisen?
oom vee feel oor moos mahn AHP rize en

How much is it?
Wie viel kostet es?
vee feel KAWS tet ess

I would like to pay my bill.
Ich möchte gerne bezahlen.
eech MERCH teh GARE neh beh TSAH len

The bill is incorrect.
Die Rechnung stimmt nicht.
dee REHCH noong shtimmt nicht

I would like to pay . . .
Ich möchte . . . bezahlen.
eech MERCH teh bay TSAH len

Ich möchte . . . bezahlen.

in cash	*bar*
	bahr
with traveler's checks	*mit Reiseschecks*
	mit RYZE eh shecks
with a credit card	*mit Kreditkarte*
	mit kray DEET kahr teh

 **Alert**

When checking into your hotel, ask whether they take credit cards and traveler's checks. Some small hotels, inns, and bed and breakfasts don't.

Chapter 6

Taking in the Town

Whether you plan to drive a rental car or use the local subway or streetcars, you need some vocabulary for transportation. In this chapter, you'll find the German terms for various types of transportation and useful phrases for getting that rental car and asking for directions.

Asking for Directions

Sometimes it's fun to wander the streets of a town or village and discover all kinds of interesting places. But if you're in a hurry, you probably ought to ask for directions.

> Where is . . . ? It's . . .
> *Wo ist . . . ? Es ist . . .*
> voe ist, ess ist

Useful Vocabulary

left	*links*
	links
right	*rechts*
	rehchts
straight (ahead)	*geradeaus*
	gheh RAH deh ows
next to	*neben*
	NAY ben
in front of	*vor*
	fore
in back of	*hinter*
	HIN tuh
above	*oben*
	OH ben
below	*unten*
	OON ten
near	*nah*
	nah
far	*weit*
	vite

in the north	*im Norden*
	im NOHR den
in the south	*im Süden*
	im ZUE den
in the east	*im Osten*
	im AWS ten
in the west	*im Westen*
	im VESS ten

 **Alert**

When making requests, like asking for directions, remember to use the polite forms and survival German vocabulary in Chapter 3.

Places to Go

Here's some vocabulary that will help you ask for directions to some important places.

Destinations

bank	*die Bank*
	dee BUNK
church	*die Kirche*
	dee KIRCH eh
city hall	*das Rathaus*
	duss RAHT hows
currency exchange	*der Geldwechsel/die Wechselstube*
	dair GHELT vex ell/
	dee VEX ell shtoo beh

hospital	*das Krankenhaus*
	duss KRAHNK en hows
movie theater	*das Kino*
	duss KEE noe
museum	*das Museum*
	duss moo ZAY oom
park	*der Park*
	dair park
pastry shop	*die Konditorei*
	dee kawn dee tore EYE
police station	*die Polizeistation*
	dee poh lee TSY shtah
	tsee OWN
post office	*das Postamt*
	duss PAWST uhmt
school	*die Schule*
	dee SHOO leh
theater	*das Theater*
	duss tay AH tuh

Other places you might like to go, including stores and businesses, are covered in Chapter 8.

⊛ ESSENTIAL Essential

Most cities have both a subway system (*die U-Bahn*) and a city and suburban train system (*die S-Bahn*). Look for the letter *U* on a sign to identify the entrance to the subway and the letter *S* that identifies the entrance to the city and suburban train.

Types of Transportation

Here are some useful words and phrases that deal with the various types of transportation.

Transportation Vocabulary

transportation	*der Transport* dare TRAHNS port
car	*der Wagen/das Auto* dare VAH gen/duss OW toe
taxi	*das Taxi* duss TAHK see
taxi stand	*der Taxistand* dare TAHK see shtunt
train	*der Zug* dare tsook
train platform	*der Bahnsteig* dare BAHN shtike
train station	*der Bahnhof* dare BAHN hofe
bus	*der Bus* dare boos
bus stop	*die Bushaltestelle* dee BOOS hult eh shtell eh
bus station	*der Busbahnhof* dare BOOS bahn hofe
subway	*die U-Bahn* dee OO bahn
subway station	*die U-Bahn-Station* dee OO bahn shtah tsee own

city and suburban train	*die S-Bahn*
	dee ESS bahn
city and suburban	*die S-Bahn-Station*
train station	dee ESS bahn shtah tsee own
bicycle	*das Fahrrad*
	duss FAHR raht
moped	*das Moped*
	duss MOE pet
boat	*das Boot*
	duss bote

 Alert

> If you use the verb *fahren* with vehicles like those listed previously, don't forget that there are two meanings for the verb. One says that you're traveling by some vehicle. The other says that you're driving that vehicle. *Ich fahre mit dem Bus.* (I'm traveling by bus.) *Ich fahre einen Bus.* (I'm driving a bus.)

Renting a Car

Public transportation is a convenient way to get around in a large city. But if you plan on traveling between cities or visiting sites out in the country, renting a car just might be the right thing for you.

I'd like to rent a car.
Ich möchte ein Auto mieten.
eech MERCH teh ine OW toe MEE ten

Vehicle Vocabulary

automatic transmission	*das Automatikgetriebe*
	duss ow toe MAH teek geh
	TREE buh
economy car	*der Economywagen*
	dare ay koe noe MEE vah gen
compact car	*der Kompaktwagen*
	dare KOME pahkt vah gen
midsize car	*der Mittelgroßwagen*
	dare MIT ell grohs vah gen
luxury car	*der Luxuswagen*
	dare LOOKS oos vah gen
convertible	*das Kabrio*
	duss KAH bree oh
four-by-four	*mit Vierradantrieb*
	mitt feer raht AHN treep
truck	*der Lastwagen*
	dare LAHST vah ghen

How much does it cost?
Wie viel kostet es?
vee feel KAWS tet ess

Do I have to pay by the kilometer?
Muss man pro Kilometer bezahlen?
moos mahn pro kee loe MAY tuh bay TSAH len

I'd like to pay by credit card.
Ich möchte mit Kreditkarte bezahlen.
eech MERCH teh mit kray DEET kahr teh beh TSAH len

Where can I pick up the car?
Wo kann ich den Wagen abholen?
voe kahn eech dane VAH ghen AHP hoe len

When do I have to return it?
Wann muss ich ihn zurückbringen?
wunn moos eech een tsoo RUECK bring en

Can I return it to Berlin/Munich?
Kann ich ihn in Berlin/München abgeben?
kahn eech een in bare LEEN/MUEN chen AHP gay ben

 Alert

Cars in Europe usually have manual transmissions, so if you can't drive a stick shift, be sure to call around to rental companies to find out who offers cars with automatic transmissions.

Car and Driver

Here's some vocabulary that every driver needs when out on the road, filling up, and finding a parking spot.

Driving Vocabulary

brake	*die Bremse*
	dee BREMZ eh
brake light	*das Bremslicht*
	duss BREMZ lihcht

drive, trip	*die Fahrt*
	dee fahrt
driver	*der Fahrer*
	dare FAHR uh
expressway	*die Autobahn*
	dee OW toe bahn
flat tire/breakdown	*die Panne*
	dee PUHN eh
gasoline	*das Benzin*
	duss ben TSEEN
gas pedal	*das Gaspedal*
	duss gahss pay DAHL
gas station	*die Tankstelle*
	dee TAHNK shtell eh
headlight	*der Scheinwerfer*
	dare SHINE vare fuh
high beam	*das Fernlicht*
	duss FAIRN lihcht
highway	*die öffentliche Straße/Landstraße*
	dee ER fent leech eh
	SHTRAH seh/LUNT shtrah seh
hitchhiking	*das Trampen*
	duss TRAHM pen
on the way	*unterwegs*
	OON tuh vakes
one-way street	*die Einbahnstraße*
	dee INE bahn shtrah seh
parking lot	*der Parkplatz*
	dare PARK plutz
regular gas	*das Normalbenzin*
	duss nore MAHL ben tseen

112

speed limit	*die Geschwindigkeitsbeschränkung*
	dee gheh SHVIN dih kites
	beh SHRENK oong
steering wheel	*das Lenkrad*
	duss LENK raht
street	*die Straße*
	dee SHTRAH seh
toll	*die Gebühr*
	dee gheh BUER
traffic jam	*der Verkehrsstau/der Stau*
	dare fare KARES shtau/
	der shtau
traffic light	*die Verkehrsampel*
	dee fare KARES ahm pell
turn signal	*der Blinker*
	dare BLINK uh
windshield	*die Windschutzscheibe*
	dee VINT shoots shy beh
windshield wiper	*der Scheibenwischer*
	dare SHY ben vish uh

ESSENTIAL Essential

The German Autobahn is famous for its convenience. Although there are places that have no speed limit, be aware that there are also areas with vigorously enforced speed limits. Be sure to keep to the right except when passing. That's a strict rule.

Useful Driving Verbs

Here are some verbs essential for driving in Germany.

Driving Verbs

to accelerate	*beschleunigen*
	beh SHLOY nih ghen
to cross	*überqueren*
	ue buh KVARE en
to drive	*fahren*
	FAHR en
to fill up (gas tank)	*tanken*
	TAHNK en
to park	*parken*
	PAHR ken
to pass	*überholen*
	UEH buh hoe len
to slow down	*verlangsamen, abbremsen*
	fare LAHNG zah men,
	AHP brem zen
to turn	*einbiegen*
	INE bee ghen

Chapter 7

Time for Dinner

Going out for dinner can be a great experience and is an important part of enjoying a foreign culture. This chapter will present you with the most essential words and phrases for understanding a German menu and ordering correctly. *Guten Appetit!*

Eating Out

Here are some basic words and phrases that you'll find helpful when eating out.

At the Restaurant

restaurant	*das Restaurant*
	duss ress toh RAHNG
snack bar	*der Schnellimbiss*
	dare SHNELL im biss
kitchen	*die Küche*
	dee KUECH eh
dining room	*das Esszimmer*
	duss ESS tsimm uh
waiter	*der Kellner*
	dare KELL nuh
waitress	*die Kellnerin*
	dee KELL nuh rin
cook	*der Koch/die Köchin*
	dare kawch/dee KERCH in

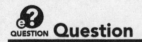 **Question**

How do I get my waiter's attention?
You can call to the waiter by saying "excuse me," *Entschuldigung* (ent SHOOL dee goong). Or you can ask for "service," *Bedienung* (beh DEEN oong).

Meals and Courses

meal	*die Mahlzeit*
	dee MAHL tsite
breakfast	*das Frühstück*
	duss FRUE shtueck
lunch	*das Mittagessen*
	duss MIT tuck ess en
dinner	*das Abendessen/Abendbrot*
	duss AH bent ess en/AH bent brote
snack	*der Snack*
	dare snack
appetizer, starter	*die Vorspeise*
	dee FORE shpy zeh
soup	*die Suppe*
	dee ZOO peh
main course	*das Hauptgericht*
	duss HOWPT gheh rihct
salad	*der Salat*
	dare zah LAHT
dessert	*der Nachtisch*
	dare NAHCH tish

What's on the Menu?

In order to choose correctly from a menu, you have to know what food items are available. Take a look at the following lists of different kinds of food.

Fruit (*das Obst*)

apple	*der Apfel*
	dare AHP fell
apricot	*die Aprikose*
	dee ahp ree KOE zeh
banana	*die Banane*
	dee bah NAH neh
blackberry	*die Brombeere*
	dee BROME bare eh
blueberry	*die Heidelbeere/Blaubeere*
	dee HYE dell bare eh/BLOU bare eh
cherry	*die Kirsche*
	dee KEER sheh
grape	*die Weintraube*
	dee VINE trow beh
grapefruit	*die Pampelmuse*
	dee PAHM pell moo zeh
lemon	*die Zitrone*
	dee tsee TRONE eh
lime	*die Limone*
	dee lee MONE eh
orange	*die Apfelsine/Orange*
	dee ahp fell ZEE neh/oh RAHN zheh
peach	*der Pfirsich*
	dare PFEER zich
pear	*die Birne*
	dee BEER neh
plum	*die Pflaume*
	dee PFLOW meh

raspberry	*die Himbeere*
	dee HIM bare eh
strawberry	*die Erdbeere*
	dee AIRT bare eh

Vegetables (*das Gemüse*)

artichoke	*die Artischocke*
	dee are tee SHOKE eh
asparagus	*der Spargel*
	dare SHPAR ghel
bean	*die Bohne*
	dee BOE neh
carrot	*die Möhre/Karotte*
	dee MER reh/kah ROTE eh
cauliflower	*der Blumenkohl*
	dare BLOOM en kole
celery	*der Stangensellerie*
	dare SHTUNG en zell air ee
corn	*der Mais*
	dare mise
cucumber	*die Gurke*
	dee GOOR keh
lettuce	*der Kopfsalat*
	dare KAWPF zah laht
mushroom	*der Pilz*
	dare piltz
onion	*die Zwiebel*
	dee TSVEE bel
parsley	*die Petersilie*
	dee pay tare ZEE lee eh

peas	*die Erbsen*
	dee AIRP sen
potato	*die Kartoffel*
	dee kahr TAWF el
spinach	*der Spinat*
	dare shpee NAHT
tomato	*die Tomate*
	dee toe MAH teh

Meat, Fish, Poultry (*das Fleisch, der Fisch, das Geflügel*)

chicken	*das Huhn/Hähnchen*
	duss hoon/HANE chen
fish	*der Fisch*
	dare fish
ham	*der Schinken*
	dare SHINK en
herring	*der Hering*
	dare HARE ing
lamb	*das Lamm*
	duss lumm
lobster	*der Hummer*
	dare HOOM uh
mussels	*die Muscheln*
	dee MOO sheln
pizza	*die Pizza*
	dee PEE tsah
pork	*das Schweinefleisch*
	duss SHVINE eh flysh
roast beef	*der Rinderbraten/das Roastbeef*
	dare RIN duh brah ten/duss roast beef

sausage	*die Wurst*
	dee voorst
steak	*das Steak*
	duss steak
turkey	*der Truthahn*
	dare TRUEHT hahn
veal	*das Kalbfleisch*
	duss KULP flysh
venison	*das Rehfleisch*
	duss RAY flysh

Meat Preparation

rare	*englisch gebraten*
	ENG lish gheh BRAH ten
medium rare/well	*halb durchgebraten*
	hulp DOORCH gheh brah ten
well done	*durchgebraten*
	DOORCH gheh brah ten

Dairy (*die Milchprodukte*)

butter	*die Butter*
	die BOOT uh
buttermilk	*die Buttermilch*
	dee BOOT uh milch
cheese	*der Käse*
	dare KAY zeh
cream	*die Sahne*
	dee ZAH neh
cream cheese	*der Frischkäse*
	dare FRISH kay zeh

curd cheese	*der Quark*
	dare kvahrk
ice cream	*das Eis*
	duss ice
milk	*die Milch*
	dee milch
sour cream	*der Sauerrahm*
	dare ZOW uh rahm
yogurt	*der Joghurt*
	dare YOGE hoort

Dessert (*der Nachtisch*)

cake	*der Kuchen*
	dare KOOCH en
candy	*die Süßigkeiten*
	dee ZUESS ich kite en
chocolate	*die Schokolade*
	dee SHOW koe lah deh
cookie	*das Plätzchen*
	duss PLETZ chen
fruit	*das Obst*
	duss ohpst
ice cream	*das Eis*
	duss ice
pie	*der Obstkuchen*
	dare OHPST kooch en
pudding	*der Pudding*
	dare POO ding

milk	*die Milch*
	dee milch
mineral water	*das Mineralwasser*
	duss minn uh RAHL vuss uh
sparkling water	*das Selterswasser*
	duss ZELL tuss vuss uh
sparkling wine,	*der Sekt*
champagne	dare zehkt
tea	*der Tee*
	dare tay
water	*das Wasser*
	duss VUSS uh
wine	*der Wein*
	dare vine

Fact

It is well known that Germans are fond of beer. That means that there are many local breweries and many kinds of beer to sample while you're enjoying a meal out. But don't be afraid to try the German wines as well. There are many fine Moselle (*Mosel*) and Rhine (*Rhein*) wines.

Dishes and Silverware

If you need to ask for another fork or a napkin, here's the vocabulary you'll need.

Dishes and Silverware (*das Geschirr und Besteck*)

bottle	*die Flasche*
	dee FLUSH eh
bowl	*die Schale*
	dee SHAH leh
butter dish, can, box	*die Dose*
	dee DOZE eh
cup	*die Tasse*
	dee TUSS eh
fork	*die Gabel*
	dee GAH bell
glass	*das Glas*
	duss glahss
highchair	*der Hochstuhl*
	dare HOECH shtool
knife	*das Messer*
	duss MESS uh
napkin	*die Serviette*
	dee zare vee ETT eh
plate	*der Teller*
	dare TELL uh
pot, jar	*der Topf*
	dare tawpf
saucer	*die Untertasse*
	dee OON tuh tuss eh
spoon	*der Löffel*
	dare LERF ell
tray	*das Tablett*
	duss tah BLETT
wineglass	*das Weinglas*
	duss VINE glahss

Ordering a Meal

With your new food and beverage vocabulary, you're ready to talk with the waiter and order your meal.

Useful Expressions

to be hungry	*Hunger haben*
	HOONG uh HAH ben
to be thirsty	*Durst haben*
	doorst HAH ben
to order	*bestellen*
	beh SHTELL en
to drink	*trinken*
	TRINK en
to eat	*essen*
	ESS en
check/bill	*die Rechnung*
	dee REHCH noong
menu	*die Speisekarte*
	dee SHPY zeh kahr teh
side order, à la carte	*à la carte*
	ah lah kart
fixed menu	*die Gedeck*
	dee gheh DECK
tip	*das Trinkgeld*
	duss TRINK ghehlt
tip (service) is included	*die Bedienung ist inbegriffen*
	dee beh DEEN oong ist in
	beh GRIFF en
tip is not included	*die Bedienung ist nicht inbegriffen*
	dee beh DEEN oong ist nihcht
	in beh GRIFF en

You can specify the kind of ethnic food you would like to eat by using the adjective that describes the nationality: *Essen wir heute mexikanisch.* (Let's go out for Mexican tonight.) *Ich esse oft chinesisch.* (I often go out for Chinese food.)

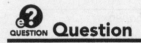 **Question**

How do I know how much of a tip to leave my server?
Gratuity is included in most restaurants. It is customary to include a service charge of 10 to 20 percent on your bill.

What would you like? I would like . . .
Was möchten Sie? Ich möchte . . .
vuss MERCH ten zee, eech MERCH teh

What are you ordering?
Was bestellen Sie?
vuss beh SHTELL en zee

I'm ordering . . .
Ich bestelle . . .
eech beh SHTELL eh

How much does . . . cost?
Wie viel kostet . . . ?
vee feel KAW stet

Enjoy your meal!
Guten Appetit!
GOO ten AHP eh teet

No smoking!
Nicht rauchen! Rauchen verboten!
nihcht ROWCH en, ROWCH en fare BOE ten

No pets allowed!
Kein Zugang für Haustiere!
KINE TSOO gung fuer HOUSE teer eh

Dietary Restrictions

While you are traveling, you can still avoid the foods that you normally would not eat at home. Use these German phrases to explain your dietary restrictions.

I am . . .
Ich bin . . .
eech bin

Useful Expressions

allergic to	*allergisch gegen*
	ah LARE gish GAY ghen
diabetic	*Diabetiker(in)*
	dee ah BET ick uh (rin)
vegetarian	*Vegetarier(in)*
	veg eh TAHR ee uh (rin)

I'm on a diet.
Ich mache eine Diät.
eech MAHCH eh INE eh dee ATE

I can't eat . . .
Ich kann kein . . . essen.
eech kahn kine . . . ESS en

Chapter 8

Shopping and Services

Vacations are fun and keep you on the go. But certain things still have to be done: You have to keep your clothes clean and your hair trimmed. And you just might be getting tired of eating in a restaurant three times a day. So this chapter will introduce you to some phrases that are related to the stores and services you might need.

Stores and Businesses

Here's a handy list of stores and businesses.

Destinations (*das Ziele*)

bakery	*die Bäckerei*
	dee beck eh RYE
bank	*die Bank*
	dee bahnk
butcher shop	*die Fleischerei/Metzgerei*
	dee flysh eh RYE/metz gheh RYE
candy shop	*das Süßwarengeschäft*
	duss ZUESS vahr en gheh sheft
clothing store	*das Bekleidungsgeschäft*
	duss beh KLY doongs gheh sheft
dairy store	*der Milchladen*
	dare MILCH lah den
department store	*das Kaufhaus*
	duss KOWF house
drugstore	*die Drogerie*
	dee droe gare EE
dry cleaner	*die chemische Reinigung*
	dee KAME ish eh RINE ee goong
fish market	*das Fischgeschäft*
	duss FISH gheh sheft
grocery store	*das Lebensmittelgeschäft*
	duss LAY bens mit tell gheh sheft
laundromat	*die Wäscherei*
	dee vesh eh RYE
mall, shopping center	*das Einkaufszentrum*
	duss INE kowfs tsen troom

newsstand	*der Zeitungskiosk*
	dare TSY toongs kee awsk
outdoor market	*der Markt*
	dare mahrkt
pastry shop	*die Konditorei*
	dee kawn dee taw RYE
pharmacy/drugstore	*die Apotheke*
	dee ah poe TAY keh
shop	*der Laden*
	dare LAH den
store	*das Geschäft*
	duss gheh SHEFT
supermarket	*der Supermarkt*
	dare SOOP uh mahrkt
tobacconist	*der Tabakwarenhändler*
	dare tah BAHK vahr en hend luh

 Fact

The *Apotheke* is one of the stores that is translated into English as "drugstore." But there is a difference between it and the *Drogerie*. In the *Drogerie*, you can obtain perfume, cosmetics, over-the-counter medicines, and various hygiene products. Some of the same products can be bought in the *Apotheke*. But the primary difference between the two is that the *Apotheke* has licensed pharmacists who can prepare prescription medicines and provide advice on their use.

Laundromat and Dry Cleaner

After traveling around for a few days, you're going to need to get your clothes cleaned. Here is some valuable vocabulary for solving this problem.

Laundry Vocabulary

bleach	*das Bleichmittel*
	duss BLYCH mit tell
detergent	*das Waschmittel*
	duss VUSH mit tell
to dry	*trocknen*
	TRAWK nen
to dry-clean	*chemisch reinigen*
	KAME ish RINE ih ghen
dryer	*der Trockner*
	dare TRAWK nuh
fabric softener	*das Weichspülmittel*
	duss VYCH shpuel mit tell
to rinse	*durchspülen*
	DOORCH shpuel en
soap	*die Seife*
	dee ZIFE eh
starch	*die Stärke*
	dee SHTARE keh
to wash	*waschen*
	VUSH en
washing machine	*die Waschmaschine*
	dee VUSH mah shee neh

Hair Salon or Barbershop

You need to know how to tell the stylist or barber how you want your hair done. Familiarize yourself with the following vocabulary.

Grooming Vocabulary

to brush	*bürsten*
	BUER sten
to blow-dry	*fönen*
	FER nen
to color	*färben*
	FARE ben
to curl	*locken*
	LAW ken
to cut	*schneiden*
	SHNY den
to perm	*eine Dauerwelle machen*
	INE eh DOW uh vell eh MAHCH en
to shave	*rasieren*
	RAH zee ren
to wash	*waschen*
	VUSH en
long	*lang*
	lung
short	*kurz*
	koortz
too cold	*zu kalt*
	tsoo kult
too hot	*zu heiß*
	tsoo hice

hairstyle	*die Frisur*
	dee free ZOOR
hair stylist	*der Friseur/die Friseuse*
	dare free ZER/dee free ZER zeh

Fact

If you bring along your own electrical appliances, such as a hair dryer or shaver, on your trip to Germany, remember that you'll need a converter. Germany, like all of Europe, has a 220-volt electrical system, different from the 110-volt system in North America.

Clothing and Jewelry

Whether you are shopping for new clothes or just folding up the laundry, the following clothing vocabulary will help you find what you need.

Clothing (*die Kleidung*)

bathing suit	*der Badeanzug*
	dare BAH deh ahn tsook
boot	*der Stiefel*
	dare SHTEE fell
coat	*der Mantel*
	dare MUHN tell
hoodie	*der Kapuzenpulli*
	dare kuh POOTS en poo lee
jacket	*die Jacke*
	dee JUCK eh

jeans	*die Jeans*
	dee jeans
pajamas	*der Schlafanzug*
	dare SHLAHF ahn tsook
pants	*die Hose*
	dee HOE zeh
raincoat	*der Regenmantel*
	dare RAY ghen muhn tell
sandals	*die Sandalen*
	dee ZAHN dah len
shoes	*die Schuhe*
	dee SHOO eh
shorts	*die kurze Hose/Shorts*
	dee KOORTS eh HOE zeh/shorts
ski jacket	*die Skijacke*
	dee SHEE yuck eh
sneakers	*die Turnschuhe*
	dee TOORN shoo eh
socks	*die Socken*
	dee ZAWK en
sweater	*der Pullover*
	dare pool OH vuh
T-shirt	*das T-Shirt*
	duss TEE shirt

Essential

Perhaps you noticed that *Hose* in German is singular, whereas in English, "pants" is plural. If *Hose* is the subject of a sentence, its verb will be singular: *Diese Hose ist zu klein.* (These pants are too small.)

Women's Clothing (*die Frauenkleidung*)

bikini	*der Bikini*
	dare bee KEE nee
blouse	*die Bluse*
	dee BLOO zeh
brassiere	*der Büstenhalter*
	dare BUE sten hult uh
dress	*das Kleid*
	duss klite
high-heeled shoes	*die hochhackigen Schuhe*
	dee HOECH huck ee ghen SHOO eh
miniskirt	*der Minirock*
	dare MINN ee rawk
nightgown	*das Nachthemd*
	duss NAHCHT hemt
panties	*der Schlüpfer*
	dare SHLUEP fuh
pantyhose, tights	*die Strumpfhose*
	dee SHTROOMPF hoe zeh
skirt	*der Rock*
	dare rawk

slip	*der Unterrock*
	dare OON tuh rawk
suit	*das Kostüm*
	duss kawss TUEM
stockings	*die Strümpfe*
	dee SHTRUEM pfeh

Men's Clothing (*die Männerkleidung*)

bow tie	*die Fliege*
	dee FLEE gheh
boxer shorts	*die Boxershorts*
	dee BAWX uh shorts
cummerbund	*der Kummerbund*
	dare KOOM uh boont
shirt	*das Hemd*
	duss hemt
sports coat	*der Sakko*
	dare ZUK oh
suit	*der Anzug*
	dare AHN tsook
tie	*der Schlips*
	dare shlips
tuxedo	*der Smoking*
	dare SMOKE ing
undershirt	*das Unterhemd*
	duss OON tuh hemt
underwear	*die Unterwäsche*
	dee OON tuh vesh eh

Jewelry (*der Schmuck*)

barrette	*die Haarspange*
	dee HAHR shpung eh
bracelet	*das Armband*
	duss AHRM bunt
brooch	*die Brosche*
	dee BRAWSH eh
charm bracelet	*das Armband mit Anhängern*
	duss AHRM bunt mit AHN heng uhn
cufflink	*der Manschettenknopf*
	dare mahn SHETT en knawpf
earring	*der Ohrring*
	dare ORE ring
engagement ring	*der Verlobungsring*
	dare fare LOE boongs ring
necklace	*die Halskette*
	dee HULSS keh teh
pendant	*der Anhänger*
	dare AHN heng uh
pin	*die Anstecknadel*
	dee AHN shteck nah dell
ring	*der Ring*
	dare ring
tie clip	*der Krawattenhalter*
	dare krah WAH ten hult uh
wedding ring	*der Ehering*
	dare AY eh ring

Accessories *(das Accessoire)*

backpack	*der Rucksack*
	dare ROOK zuck
belt	*der Gürtel*
	dare GUER tell
briefcase	*die Aktentasche*
	dee AHK ten tush eh
eyeglasses	*die Brille*
	dee BRILL eh
gloves	*die Handschuhe*
	dee HUNT shoo eh
handkerchief	*das Taschentuch*
	duss TUSH en tooch
hat	*der Hut*
	dare hoot
mittens	*die Fausthandschuhe*
	dee FOWST hunt shoo eh
neckerchief, scarf	*das Halstuch*
	duss HULLS tooch
purse	*die Handtasche*
	dee HUNT tush eh
ribbon	*das Band*
	duss bunt
scarf, muffler	*der Schal*
	dare shahl
shawl	*das Schultertuch*
	duss SHOOL tuh tooch
sunglasses	*die Sonnenbrille*
	dee ZAWN en brill eh
umbrella	*der Regenschirm*
	dare RAY ghen shirm

wallet   *die Brieftasche*
                dee BREEF tush eh

Colors and Sizes

Since colors are adjectives, refer to Chapter 2 for a review
of how adjective endings work in German.

Colors (*die Farben*)

purple	*lila/violett*
	LEE lah/vee oh LET
blue	*blau*
	blou (rhymes with "wow")
green	*grün*
	gruen
yellow	*gelb*
	ghelp
orange	*orange*
	oh RAWN zhe
red	*rot*
	rote
black	*schwarz*
	shvahrtz
white	*weiß*
	vice
gray	*grau*
	grow
brown	*braun*
	brown
pink	*rosa*
	ROH zah

light blue	*hellblau*
	HELL blou
dark blue	*dunkelblau*
	DOONK ell blou

Sizes (*die Größen*)

clothing size	*die Kleidergröße*
	dee KLY duh grer seh
shoe size	*die Schuhgröße*
	dee SHOO grer seh

What size do you wear? I wear size . . .
Welche Größe tragen Sie? Ich trage Größe . . .
VELL cheh GRER seh TRAH ghen zee, eech TRAH gheh
grer seh . . .

German clothing and shoe sizes are numbered according
to a system different from the British and American system, so
you'll need to find a chart of equivalents. If you try something
on that doesn't fit, the following vocabulary will be helpful.

Useful Expressions

large	*groß*
	groess
larger	*größer*
	GRERE suh
medium	*mittelgroß*
	MIT ell groess
small	*klein*
	kline
smaller	*kleiner*
	KLINE uh

Chapter 9

Activities and Entertainment

You've done a little shopping, found some new things to buy, and even got a haircut. Now you're ready to go out on the town and do some exploring or have some fun. You can take in a movie or a play, or perhaps go hear a concert. But in order to do these things, you'll need some vocabulary to see you through.

Verbs When You're a Participant

Let's look at the verbs *machen* (to do/make) and *spielen* (to play), which will be helpful when you're involved in an activity.

The Verb *Machen*

	Present/Past
ich	*mache* [MAHCH eh]
	machte [MAHCH teh]
du	*machst* [mahchst]
	machtest [MAHCH test]
er, sie, es	*macht* [mahcht]
	machte [MAHCH teh]
wir	*machen* [MAHCH en]
	machten [MAHCH ten]
ihr	*macht* [mahcht]
	machtet [MAHCH tet]
Sie	*machen* [MAHCH en]
	machten [MAHCH ten]
sie	*machen* [MAHCH en]
	machten [MAHCH ten]

What are you doing?
Was machen Sie?
vuss MAHCH en zee

I'm making the bed.
Ich mache das Bett.
eech MAHCH eh duss bet

The verb *machen* is used in many idiomatic expressions that cannot be translated word for word into English. Such expressions must simply be learned and used when appropriate. Let's look at a few useful examples.

Make yourself comfortable/at home.
Mach es dir gemütlich.
mahch ess deer gheh MUET lich

Hurry up!
Mach schnell!
mahch shnell

Never mind. It doesn't matter.
Macht nichts.
mahcht nihchtz

The Verb *Spielen*

	Present/Past
ich	*spiele* [SHPEEL eh]
	spielte [SHPEEL teh]
du	*spielst* [shpeelst]
	spieltest [SHPEEL test]
er, sie, es	*spielt* [shpeelt]
	spielte [SHPEEL teh]
wir	*spielen* [SHPEEL en]
	spielten [SHPEEL ten]
ihr	*spielt* [shpeelt]
	spieltet [SHPEEL tet]
Sie	*spielen* [SHPEEL en]
	spielten [SHPEEL ten]

| sie | *spielen* [SHPEEL en] |
| | *spielten* [SHPEEL ten] |

The verb *spielen* is used very much like its English equivalent "to play": You play sports, games, and musical instruments. And just like English, German doesn't need any prepositions following this verb. The sports, games, and instruments are all direct objects.

Do you play tennis?
Spielen Sie Tennis?
SHPEEL en zee TEN iss

We're playing chess.
Wir spielen Schach.
veer SHPEEL en shuch

My daughter plays piano.
Meine Tochter spielt Klavier.
MINE eh TAWCH tuh shpeel KLUH vee uh

 **ESSENTIAL Essential**

Notice that, just like English, German doesn't always require a definite article with the name of a sport, game, or musical instrument: *Mein Sohn spielt Geige.* (My son plays [the] violin.)

Verbs When You're a Spectator

Two important verbs that allow you to be a spectator are *sehen* (to see) and *hören* (to hear).

The Verb *Sehen*

	Present/Past
ich	*sehe* [ZAY eh]
	sah [zah]
du	*siehst* [zeest]
	sahst [zahst]
er, sie, es	*sieht* [zeet]
	sah [zah]
wir	*sehen* [ZAY en]
	sahen [ZAH en]
ihr	*seht* [zate]
	saht [zaht]
Sie	*sehen* [ZAY en]
	sahen [ZAH en]
sie	*sehen* [ZAY en]
	sahen [ZAH en]

I saw the children playing in the yard.
Ich sah die Kinder im Garten spielen.
eech zah dee KINN duh im GAHR ten SHPEEL en

She sees a pretty bird.
Sie sieht einen schönen Vogel.
zee zeet INE en SHERN en FOE ghel

147

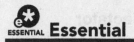

In some special phrases the verb *sehen* can have a different meaning in English: *Ich sehe fern.* (I'm watching TV.) *Sieh mal!* (Look!)

The Verb *Hören*

Present/Past

ich	*höre* [HER eh]
	hörte [HER teh]
du	*hörst* [herst]
	hörtest [HER test]
er, sie, es	*hört* [hert]
	hörte [HER teh]
wir	*hören* [HER en]
	hörten [HER ten]
ihr	*hört* [hert]
	hörtet [HER tet]
Sie	*hören* [HER en]
	hörten [HER ten]
sie	*hören* [HER en]
	hörten [HER ten]

We hear the children singing.
Wir hören die Kinder singen.
veer HER en dee KINN duh ZING en

Do you hear the beautiful music?
Hören Sie die schöne Musik?
HER en zee dee SHERN eh moo ZEEK

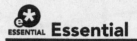 **Essential**

> In some special phrases the verb *hören* can have a different meaning in English: *Ich höre Radio.* (I'm listening to the radio.) *Lass mal etwas von dir hören!* (Keep in touch!)

Sports and Games

You can use the verb spielen when talking about the following sports and games.

Sports and Games Vocabulary

baseball	*der Baseball*
	dare BASE bul
basketball	*der Basketball/Korbball*
	dare BASS ket bul/KAWRP bul
cards	*die Karten*
	dee KAHR ten
chess	*das Schach*
	duss shuch
computer game	*das Computerspiel*
	duss kom PYOO tuh shpeel
golf	*das Golf*
	duss gawlf
hockey	*das Hockey*
	duss HAWK ee
soccer	*der Fußball*
	dare FOOSS bul

tennis	*das Tennis*
	duss TEN iss
volleyball	*der Volleyball*
	dare VAWL ee bul

Alert

Notice that *Fußball* means "football" in British English but in American English it's "soccer." The Germans call American football *der amerikanische Football*.

The verb *gehen* (to go) is used when participating in a variety of other sports and activities.

	Present	**Past**
ich	*gehe* [GAY eh]	*ging* [ghing]
du	*gehst* [gayst]	*gingst* [ghingst]
er, sie, es	*geht* [GATE]	*ging* [ghing]
wir	*gehen* [GAY en]	*gingen* [GHING en]
ihr	*geht* [gate]	*gingt* [ghingt]
Sie	*gehen* [GAY en]	*gingen* [GHING en]
sie	*gehen* [GAY en]	*gingen* [GHING en]

Are you going biking?
Gehst du radfahren?
gayst doo RAHT fahr en

No, I'm going for a walk.
Nein, ich gehe spazieren.
nine eech GAY eh SHPUH tseer en

Useful Verbs

to hike	*wandern*
	VUN dairn
to jog	*joggen*
	JAW ghen
to roller-skate	*Rollschuh laufen*
	RAWL shoo low fen
to row	*rudern*
	ROO dairn
to sail	*segeln*
	ZAY gheln
to ski	*Ski laufen*
	shee LOW fen
to stroll	*bummeln*
	BOOM eln
to surf	*surfen*
	ZOOR fen
to swim	*schwimmen*
	SHVIM en
to water ski	*Wasserski laufen*
	VUSS uh shee low fen

Hobbies

The following vocabulary will be helpful when you speak about hobbies with someone.

cooking/to cook	*das Kochen/kochen*
	duss KAWCH en
dancing/to dance	*das Tanzen/tanzen*
	duss TAHNTS en
fishing/to fish	*das Angeln/angeln*
	duss AHNG eln
to go fishing	*fischen gehen/angeln gehen*
	FISH en GAY en/AHNG eln GAY en
gardening	*die Gartenarbeit*
	dee GAHR ten ahr bite
to garden	*im Garten arbeiten/gärtnern*
	im GAHR ten AHR bite en
hunting/to hunt	*die Jagd/jagen*
	dee YAHKT/YAH ghen
music	*die Musik*
	dee moo ZEEK
to listen to music	*Musik hören*
	moo ZEEK HER en
to play music	*Musik spielen*
	moo ZEEK SHPEEL en
flute	*die Flöte*
	dee FLER teh
guitar	*die Gitarre*
	dee GHEE tahr eh
organ	*die Orgel*
	dee AWR ghel
piano	*das Klavier*
	duss KLAH veer
trumpet	*die Trompete*

	dee TROME pay teh
violin	*die Geige*
	dee GYE gheh
reading/to read	*das Lesen/lesen*
	duss LAY zen

Movies and Television

Other ways of enjoying a variety of entertainment types are going to the movies and watching television. Here's some useful vocabulary for these venues.

Movie and Television Vocabulary

movie	*der Film*
	dare film
feature film	*der Spielfilm*
	dare SHPEEL film
to watch a movie	*sich einen Film ansehen*
	zeech INE en film AHN zay en
movie theater	*das Kino*
	duss KEE noe
presentation	*die Vorstellung/Vorführung*
	dee FORE shtell oong/FORE fuer oong
seat	*der Platz*
	dare plutz
television	*das Fernsehen*
	duss FAIRN zay en
to watch television	*fernsehen*
	FAIRN zay en
television show	*die Fernsehsendung*
	dee FAIRN zay zen doong

153

dubbed	*synchronisiert*
	zuen kroe nee ZEERT
subtitled	*mit Untertiteln*
	mit OON tuh tee teln

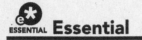 **Essential**

> The verb *fernsehen* is used differently from its English equivalent "to watch television." The prefix *fern-* is placed at the end of the sentence and the word "television" doesn't even appear in the sentence: *Wir sehen jeden Abend fern.* (We watch television every evening.) *Siehst du schon wieder fern?* (Are you watching television again?)

Going to the Theater

Use the following vocabulary for live performances.

Theater Vocabulary

theater	*das Theater*
	duss TAY ah tuh
opera	*die Oper*
	dee OH puh
symphony	*die Sinfonie*
	dee zeen foe NEE
concert	*das Konzert*
	duss KONE tsairt

ballet	*das Ballett*
	duss buh LET
performance	*die Aufführung/Vorstellung*
	dee OW fuer oong/FORE shtell oong
balcony	*der Balkon*
	dare buhl KONE
box	*die Loge*
	dee LOE zheh
orchestra	*das Orchester*
	duss ore KESS tuh

Chapter 10

German for Business

Knowing some German business vocabulary can come in handy, particularly if you plan to work in Germany or deal with people who do. This chapter will provide you with words and phrases about professions, work situations, office equipment, banking, changing money, and school.

Jobs and Professions

Most nouns that describe professions have a masculine and feminine form that are identical except for the feminine *–in* ending, for example *der Lehrer/die Lehrerin* (teacher). Where the masculine and feminine in the following lists are identical, the feminine will be identified by the ending *–in*. If the feminine form is different from the masculine, the entire word will be provided for you.

Professions (*der Berufe*)

actor	*der Schauspieler/die –in*
	dare SHAU shpeel uh/dee in
artist	*der Künstler/die –in*
	dare KUENST luh/dee in
baker	*der Bäcker/die –in*
	dare BECK un/dee in
butcher	*der Fleischer/die –in*
	dare FLY shuh/dee in
carpenter	*der Tischler/die –in*
	dare TISH luh/dee in
civil servant	*der Beamte/die Beamtin*
	dare bay UHM teh/dee bay UM tin
cook	*der Koch/die Köchin*
	dare kawch/dee KERCH in
dentist	*der Zahnarzt/die Zahnärztin*
	dare TSAHN ahrtst/dee TSAHN-airts tin
doctor	*der Arzt/die Ärztin*
	dare ahrtst/dee AIRTS tin
doorman	*der Pförtner/die –in*
	dare PFERT nuh/dee in

electrician	*der Elektriker/die –in*
	dare ay LECK tree kuh/dee in
employee	*der/die Angestellte*
	dare/dee AHN gheh shtell teh
engineer	*der Ingenieur/die –in*
	dare een zheh NEUR/dee in
fireman	*der Feuerwehrmann/*
	die Feuerwehrfrau
	dare FOY uh vare mun/dee FOY
	uh vare frow
lawyer/attorney	*der Rechtsanwalt/*
	die Rechtsanwältin
	dare REHCHTS ahn vahlt/
	dee REHCHTS ahn velt in
maid	*das Dienstmädchen*
	duss DEENST mate chen
manager	*der Manager/die –in*
	dare MEN uh juh/die in
mechanic	*der Mechaniker/die –in*
	dare may CHAHN ee kuh/dee in
nurse	*der Krankenpfleger* (m.)/
	die Krankenschwester (f.)
	dare KRUNK en pflay guh/
	dee KRUNK en shvess tuh
pharmacist	*der Apotheker/die –in*
	dare AH poe tay kuh/dee in
plumber	*der Klempner/die –in*
	dare KLEMP nuh/dee in
police officer	*der Polizist/die –in*
	dare po lee TSIST/dee in

professor	*der Professor/die –in*
	dare pro FESS or/dee in
receptionist (hotel)	*der Empfangschef/*
	die Empfangsdame
	dare emp FUNGS sheff/
	dee emp FUNGS dah meh
secretary	*der Sekretär/die –in*
	dare zeh kray TARE/dee in
student	*der Student/die –in*
	dare shtoo DENT/dee in
waiter/server	*der Kellner/die –in*
	dare KELL nuh/dee in
writer	*der Schriftsteller/die –in*
	dare SHRIFT shtell uh/dee in

FACT **Fact**

> Germans make a distinction between students in early
> grades and students at the university level. Pre-college
> pupils are called *Schüler* and *Schülerin*. University-
> level students are called *Student* and *Studentin*.

German in the Workplace

To get along in the German workplace, you need some
basic vocabulary that deals with people in various posi-
tions, employment, and earnings.

Workplace Vocabulary

boss	*der Chef/die –in*
	dare sheff/dee in
business card	*die Geschäftskarte*
	dee gheh SHEFTS kahr teh
CEO	*der Generaldirektor/die –in*
	dare ghen air AHL dee RECK tor/
	dee in
company	*die Firma*
	dee FEER mah
contract	*der Vertrag*
	dare fare TRAHK
employment	*die Arbeit*
	dee AHR bite
interview	*das Vorstellungsgespräch*
	duss FORE shtell oongs gheh
	SHPRAYCH
job	*der Job*
	dare jawp
meeting	*das Treffen*
	duss TREFF en
minimum wage	*der Mindestlohn*
	dare MIN dest lone
raise	*die Lohnerhöhung*
	dee LONE air her oong
resume	*der Lebenslauf*
	dare LAY bens lowf
salary, wage	*der Lohn*
	dare lone
unemployed	*arbeitslos*
	AHR bites loes

to apply for a job	*sich bei einer Firma bewerben*
	zeech by INE uh FEAR muh beh
	VARE ben
to fire	*entlassen*
	ent LUSS en
to hire	*einstellen*
	INE shtell en
to lay off	*vorübergehend entlassen*
	fore UEB uh gay ent ent LUSS en

On the Phone

Speaking on the phone in a foreign language is a daunting experience. Not being able to see the person you're speaking to seems to make comprehension that much more difficult. When someone answers the phone, he or she is most likely to say *hallo* (hah LOE). But many answer with a last name such as Keller ("Keller speaking"). The following phrases will help you through your calls.

May I speak to . . . ?
Kann ich . . . sprechen?
kahn eech SHPREHCH en

I'd like to speak to . . .
Ich möchte . . . sprechen.
eech MERCH teh SHPREHCH en

Who is calling? This is . . .
Wer ruft an? Hier spricht . . .
vare rooft ahn heer shpricht

Don't hang up.
Bleiben Sie am Apparat!
BLY ben zee ahm ahp ah RAHT

I'll connect you.
Ich verbinde Sie.
eech fare BIN deh zee

The line is busy.
Die Leitung ist besetzt.
dee LYE toong ist beh ZEHTZT

Telephone Vocabulary

phone number	*die Telefonnummer*
	dee tay lay fone NOO muh
area code	*die Vorwahl*
	dee FORE vahl
phone book	*das Telefonbuch*
	duss tay lay fone BOOCH
mobile/cell phone	*das Mobiltelefon/Handy*
	duss moe beel tay lay FONE/
	HEN dee
dial tone	*der Wählton*
	dare VALE tone
collect call	*das R-Gespräch*
	duss AIR gheh shpraych
local call	*das Ortsgespräch*
	duss OHRTS gheh shpraych
long-distance call	*das Ferngespräch*
	duss FAIRN gheh shpraych

answering machine	*der Anrufbeantworter*
	dare AHN roof beh ahnt vawr tuh
to call	*anrufen/telefonieren*
	AHN roof fen/tay lay foe NEER en
to call back	*wieder anrufen*
	VEE duh AHN roof en
to be cut off	*unterbrochen werden*
	oont uh BRAWCH en VARE den
to dial a number	*eine Nummer wählen*
	INE eh NOO muh VAY len
to hang up	*aufhängen*
	OWF heng en
to leave a message	*eine Nachricht hinterlassen*
	INE eh NAHCH richt HIN tuh luss en
to pick up the phone	*den Hörer abnehmen*
	dane HER uh AHP nay men
to ring	*klingeln*
	KLING eln

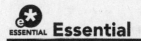

Essential

When completing a telephone call, you shouldn't use the expression *auf Wiedersehen* to say good-bye. Instead, say *auf Wiederhören*, which is something like "until I hear from you again."

Office Supplies and Equipment

You won't get any work done if you don't have the right supplies and equipment. Use the following German vocabulary to equip your office.

Office Vocabulary

desk	*der Schreibtisch*
	dare SHRIPE tish
inbox	*der Posteingang*
	dare PAWST ine gung
put in the outbox	*in die Post legen*
	in dee PAWST LAY ghen
(fountain) pen	*der Füller*
	dare FUE luh
pencil	*der Bleistift*
	dare BLY shtift
highlighter	*der Textmarker*
	dare TEXT mahr kuh
stapler	*der Hefter*
	dare HEFF tuh
staple	*die Heftklammer*
	dee HEFT klum uh
paper clip	*die Büroklammer*
	dee bue ROE klum uh
paper	*das Papier*
	duss puh PEER
piece of paper	*das Stück Papier*
	duss shtueck puh PEER
filing cabinet	*der Aktenschrank*
	dare AHK ten shrunk

file folder	*die Mappe*
	dee MUP eh
computer	*der Computer*
	dare kawm PYOO tuh
printer	*der Drucker*
	dare DROO kuh
copy machine	*das Kopiergerät*
	duss koe PEER gheh rate
fax machine	*das Faxgerät*
	duss FEX gheh rate
scanner	*der Scanner*
	dair SCANN uh
USB cable	der USB Kabel
	dair oo ess bay KAH bel
typewriter	*die Schreibmaschine*
	dee SHRIPE muh shee neh
calculator	*der Rechner*
	dare REHCH nuh
telephone	*das Telefon*
	duss tay lay FONE
e-mail	*die E-Mail*
	dee EE male

 Fact

You have to know how to use the equipment in your office. The German verb "to use" is *benutzen* (beh NOOTZ en). The verb "repair" is *reparieren* (ray pahr EER en). "To turn on" and "to turn off" are *anschalten* (AHN shul ten) and *abschalten* (AHP shul ten) respectively.

Banking and Changing Money

Money is important in everyday life and no less significant when traveling. Therefore, it's essential to know the vocabulary that will help you indicate your preferred method of payment, change money, and deal with bank accounts.

Banking Vocabulary

money	*das Geld*
	duss ghelt
bill, paper money	*der Geldschein*
	dare GHELT shine
cash	*das Bargeld*
	duss BAHR ghelt
change	*das Kleingeld*
	duss KLINE ghelt
coin	*die Münze*
	dee MUEN tseh
check	*der Scheck*
	dare sheck
checkbook	*das Scheckbuch*
	duss SHECK booch
certified check	*der bestätigte Scheck*
	dare beh SHTATE ick tuh sheck
traveler's check	*der Reisescheck*
	dare RYE zeh sheck
bank card/ATM card	*Die Bankkarte*
	dee BUNK kahr teh
credit card	*die Kreditkarte*
	dee kray DEET kahr teh

debit card	*die Debitkarte/Kundenkarte*
	dee deh BEET kahr teh/
	KOON den kahr teh
bank	*die Bank*
	dee bunk
savings bank	*die Sparkasse*
	dee SHPAHR kuss eh
ATM/cash dispenser	*der Geldautomat*
	dare GHELT ow toe maht
checking account	*das Girokonto*
	duss GHEE roe kawn toe
savings account	*das Sparkonto*
	duss SHPAHR kawn toe
balance	*der Kontostand*
	dare KAWN toe shtunt
bank statement	*der Kontoauszug*
	dare KAWN toe ows tsook
exchange rate	*der Wechselkurs*
	dare VEX ell koors
fee	*die Gebühr*
	dee gheh BUER
interest rate	*der Zinssatz*
	dare TSINZ zutz
loan	*das Darlehen*
	duss DAHR lay en
receipt	*die Quittung*
	dee KVIT oong
sum/total	*die Summe/der Betrag*
	dee ZOOM eh/dare beh TRAHK
gain, yield	*der Ertrag*
	dare air TRAHK

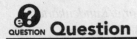

Question

Are there other places besides a bank where I can change money?
There are usually money exchange offices at border crossings, large railroad stations, and airports. They're usually open beyond the regular hours of banks and savings banks, which is generally weekdays from 8 A.M. to 12:30 P.M. and then from 2:30 P.M. until 4 P.M. When looking for money exchange offices, watch for signs that say *Wechselstube* (VEX ell shtoo beh) or *Geldwechsel* (GHELT vex ell).

Banking Verbs

to buy	*kaufen*
	KOW fen
to cash a check	*einen Scheck einlösen*
	INE en sheck INE ler zen
to change money	*Geld (in Euro) wechseln*
(into euros)	ghelt (in OY roe) VEX eln
to count	*zählen*
	TSAY len
to deposit	*einzahlen*
	INE tsah len
to earn	*verdienen*
	fair deen en
to need	*brauchen*
	BROW chen

to pay	*bezahlen*
	beh TSAH len
to save money	*Geld sparen*
	ghelt SHPAH ren
to sell	*verkaufen*
	fare KOW fen
to sign	*unterschreiben*
	oon tuh SHRIBE en
to spend	*ausgeben*
	OWS gay ben
to write a check	*einen Scheck schreiben*
	INE en sheck SHRY ben
to withdraw	*(von einem Konto) abheben*
(from an account)	(fawn INE em KAWN toe) AHP
	hay ben

In School

If you plan on taking some classes or are dealing with someone who is, you'll find the following vocabulary related to schools useful.

Education Vocabulary

school	*die Schule*
	dee SHOO leh
elementary school	*die Grundschule*
	dee GROONT shoo leh
high school	*das Gymnasium*
	duss ghuem NAHZ ee oom
university	*die Universität*
	dee oo nee vare see TATE

backpack	*der Rucksack*
	dare ROOK zahk
binder	*die Ringmappe*
	dee ring mup eh
book	*das Buch*
	duss BOOCH
chalk	*die Kreide*
	dee KRY deh
chalkboard	*die Wandtafel*
	dee VAHNT tah fell
classroom	*das Klassenzimmer*
	duss KLUSS en tsim uh
subject	*das Fach*
	duss fahch
department	*die Fakultät*
	dee fah kool TATE
dictionary	*das Wörterbuch*
	duss VER tuh booch
eraser	*der Radiergummi*
	dare rah DEER goo mee
grade (year in school)	*die Klasse*
	dee KLUSS eh
grade, mark	*die Note*
	dee NOE teh
homework	*die Schularbeit, die Hausaufgaben*
	dee SHOOL ahr bite,
	dee house owf gah ben
kindergarten	*der Kindergarten*
	dare KIN duh gahr ten

laptop	*der Laptop/tragbare PC*
	dare LEP tope/TRAHG bah re pay tsay
major (main subject)	*das Hauptfach*
	duss HOWPT fahch
map	*die Landkarte*
	dee LUNT kahr teh
notebook	*das Heft*
	duss heft
paper	*das Papier*
	duss pah PEER
piece of paper	*das Stück Papier*
	duss shtueck pah PEER
student desk	*der Tisch*
	dare tish
exam	*das Examen*
	duss ex AH men
general diploma	*der Schulabschluss*
	dare shool ahp shloos
high-school diploma	*das Abitur*
	duss ah bee TOOR
to enroll (at a university)	*immatrikulieren*
	im mah tree koo LEER en
to earn a doctorate	*promovieren*
	proe moe VEER en
to habilitate,	*habilitieren*
qualify as a professor	hah bee lee TEER en
doctorate	*der Doktorgrad*
	dare DAWK tawr graht

Chapter 11

German Medical Phrases

In case you need to go to a doctor or dentist or find a police station while traveling, these German words and phrases that deal with illness, medicine, and emergencies will come in handy.

Common Ailments

This German vocabulary deals with common ailments. These phrases can help you get the proper medical assistance when needed. The following vocabulary goes with *haben* (to have). For example, "to have arthritis" is *Arthritis haben*.

Medical Vocabulary with *Haben*

arthritis	*Arthritis*
	ahrt REE tees
a cold	*eine Erkältung*
	INE eh air KELL toong
diarrhea	*Durchfall*
	DOORCH fuhl
an earache	*eine Ohrenschmerzen*
	INE eh OH rehn shmairtz en
a fever	*ein Fieber*
	ine FEE buh
the flu	*die Grippe*
	dee GRIP peh
frostbite	*Erfrierungen*
	air FREER oong en
hay fever	*Heuschnupfen*
	HOY shnoop fen
a headache	*eine Kopfschmerzen*
	INE eh KAWPF shmairtz en
heartburn	*Sodbrennen*
	ZOHT brenn en
hemorrhoids	*Hämorrhoiden*
	hay more HOY den

a runny nose	*eine laufende Nase*
	INE eh LOW fehn deh NAH zeh
sciatica	*Ischias*
	ISH ee us
seasickness	*die Seekrankheit*
	dee ZAY krunk hite
sinusitis	*Sinusitis*
	zee noo ZEE tees
a stomachache	*eine Magenschmerzen*
	INE eh MAH ghen shmairtz en

Another group of illnesses is expressed using the verb *sein* (to be). For example, "to be asthmatic" is *Asthmatiker sein*.

Medical Vocabulary with *Sein*

asthmatic	*Asthmatiker/asthmatisch*
	AHST mah tee kuh/AHST mah tish
carsick	*autokrank*
	OW toe krunk
(have) a cold	*erkältet (sein)*
	air KELL tet
diabetic	*Diabetiker/diabetisch*
	dee ah BATE ee kuh/dee ah BATE ish

There is one term that is unique. If you wish to say you are an insomniac, use the phrase *Ich leide an Schlaflosigkeit* (eech LYE deh ahn SHLAHF loze ik kite).

Medical Verbs

to need an inhaler
einen Inhalationsapparat brauchen
INE en in hah lah tsee OWNS ahp ah raht BROW chen

to need sugar now
Zucker sofort brauchen
TSOO kuh zoe FORT BROW chen

to have high blood pressure
hohen Blutdruck haben
HOE en BLOOT drook HAH ben

to have low blood pressure
niedrigen Blutdruck haben
NEE dree ghen BLOOT drook HAH ben

to break one's arm/leg
sich den Arm/das Bein brechen
zeech dane ahrm/duss bine BREHCH en

 Alert

Unlike English, German doesn't use possessive adjectives with parts of the body, such as "my arm" or "her leg." Instead, reflexive pronouns are used and the body part is preceded by a definite article (*der, die, das*): *Er bricht sich den Finger.* (He breaks his finger.)

Parts of the Body

Whether you are in a doctor's office or a clothing store, knowing the parts of the body is useful.

Parts of the Body (*die Körperteile*)

hair	*das Haar*
	duss hahr
head	*der Kopf*
	dare kawpf
face	*das Gesicht*
	duss gheh ZIHCHT
eye	*das Auge*
	duss OW gheh
eyes	*die Augen*
	dee OW ghen
nose	*die Nase*
	dee NAH zeh
cheek	*die Backe/Wange*
	dee BUCK eh/VUNG eh
mouth	*der Mund*
	dare moont
lip	*die Lippe*
	dee LIP eh
tooth	*der Zahn*
	dare tsahn
ear	*das Ohr*
	duss ore
neck	*der Hals*
	dare huhls
chest	*die Brust*
	dee broost

stomach	*der Magen*
	dare MAH ghen
arm	*der Arm*
	dare ahrm
shoulder	*die Schulter*
	dee SHOOL tuh
elbow	*der Ellbogen*
	dare ELL boe ghen
wrist	*das Handgelenk*
	duss HUNT gheh lenk
hand	*die Hand*
	dee hunt
finger	*der Finger*
	dare FEENG uh
fingernail	*der Fingernagel*
	dare FEENG uh nah ghel
thumb	*der Daumen*
	dare DOW men
back	*der Rücken*
	dare RUE ken
leg	*das Bein*
	duss bine
knee	*das Knie*
	duss knee
ankle	*das Fußgelenk*
	duss FOOS gheh lenk
foot	*der Fuß*
	dare foos
toe	*der Zeh*
	dare tsay

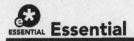

ESSENTIAL Essential

The words *Backe* and *Wange* tend to be used for the cheeks of the face. If you wish to refer to the "cheek" of the buttocks, you should use the term *die Hinterbacke* (dee HIN tuh buck uh).

Going to the Doctor

If you need to go the doctor while traveling, use the following vocabulary along with the common ailments already presented to describe your symptoms.

I'm cold. (I feel cold.)
Mir ist kalt.
meer ist kult

I'm hot. (I feel hot.)
Mir ist heiß.
meer ist hice

He's dizzy. (He feels dizzy.)
Ihm ist schwindlig.
eem ist SHVIND lik

I'm jet-lagged.
Mir macht die Zeitumstellung zu schaffen.
meer mahcht dee TSITE oom shtell oong tsoo SHUFF en

You can use the verb *sein* (to be) with many adjectives that express how you feel.

I am ...
Ich bin ...
eech bin

Ich bin ...

seasick	*seekrank*
	ZAY krunk
pregnant	*schwanger*
	SHVUNG uh
sick	*krank*
	krunk
tired	*müde*
	MUE deh

I'm constipated.
Ich leide an Verstopfung.
eech LYE deh ahn fare SHTAWP foong

He's sunburned.
Er hat einen Sonnenbrand.
air haht INE en ZAWN en brahnt

I'm allergic to ...
Ich bin gegen ... allergisch.
eech bin GAY ghen ... ull AIR gish

Ich bin gegen ... allergisch.

aspirin	*Aspirin*
	ah spee REEN
iodine	*Jod*
	yote

| penicillin | *Penizillin* |
| | pay nee tsee LEEN |

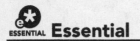

Essential

Review Chapter 7 if you are allergic to foods. You can also say that you're allergic to something by using the phrase *Ich bin Allergiker.* (I'm an allergy sufferer.)

Symptomatic Verbs

ache	*weh tun*
	vay toon
to bleed	*bluten*
	BLOO ten
to faint	*in Ohnmacht fallen*
	in OWN mahcht FUHL en
to fall	*fallen*
	FUHL en
to limp	*hinken*
	HINK en
to sneeze	*niesen*
	NEEZ en
to throw up	*sich erbrechen*
	zeech air BREHCH en

Going to the Dentist

Should you need to see a dentist while traveling, you want
to be sure you can communicate your problems. Here is
some essential German vocabulary that will be helpful.

Dental Vocabulary

at the dentist's office	*beim Zahnarzt*
	bime TSAHN ahrtst
tooth	*der Zahn*
	dare tsahn
baby tooth	*der Milchzahn*
	dare MIHLCH tsahn
back tooth	*der Backenzahn ganz hinten*
	dare bahk en tsahn gahnts hin ten
canine tooth	*der Eckzahn*
	dare ECK tsahn
front tooth	*der vordere Zahn*
	dare FORE dare eh tsahn
lower tooth	*der untere Zahn*
	dare OON tare eh tsahn
molar	*der Backenzahn*
	dare BUCK en tsahn
upper tooth	*der obere Zahn*
	dare OH bare eh tsahn
wisdom tooth	*der Weisheitszahn*
	dare VICE hites tsahn
gums	*das Zahnfleisch*
	duss TSAHN flysh
jaw	*der Kiefer*
	dare KEE fuh

mouth	*der Mund*
	dare moont
abscess	*der Abszess*
	dare ahp TSESS
toothache	*das Zahnweh*
	duss TSAHN vay
local anesthesia	*die örtliche Betäubung*
	dee ERT lich eh beh TOY boong
a broken tooth	*ein abgebrochener Zahn*
	ine AHP gheh brawch en uh tsahn
cavity	*das Loch*
	duss lawch
crown	*die Zahnkrone*
	dee TSAHN kroe neh
filling	*die Zahnfüllung*
	dee TSAHN fuell oong
infected	*infiziert*
	in fee TSEERT
injection	*die Injektion/Spritze*
	dee in yeck tsee OWN/SHPRITZ eh
anesthetic	*das Betäubungsmittel*
	duss beh TOY boongs mit tell
open your mouth	*machen Sie den Mund auf*
	MAHCH en zee dane moont owf
root canal	*die Wurzelbehandlung*
	dee VOOR tsell beh hahnd loong
teeth cleaning	*die Zahnreinigung*
	dee TSAHN rine ee goong
dental floss	*die Zahnseide*
	dee TSAHN zye deh

toothbrush	*die Zahnbürste*
	dee TSAHN buers teh
dentures	*die Zahnprothese*
	dee TSAHN pro tay zeh

A Few Dental Verbs

to bleed	*bluten*
	BLOOT en
to brush one's teeth	*sich die Zähne putzen*
	zeech dee TSAY neh POOTZ en
to injure	*verletzen*
	FARE letz en
to lose	*verlieren*
	FARE lee ren
to pull out, extract	*extrahieren, ausziehen*
	ex trah HEE ren, OWS tsee en
to replace	*ersetzen*
	air ZETZ en
to rinse out	*ausspülen*
	OWS shpue len

Fact

The German preposition *bei* is translated as "by" or "at" in English. It is also translated as "at a person's home," "at someone's office," or "for a certain employer." For example, *bei Frau Keller* (at Mrs. Keller's house), *beim Arzt* (at the doctor's office), and *bei einer Bank arbeiten* (to work for a bank).

Going to the Pharmacy

The following list of words and phrases will come in handy when you pay a visit to a pharmacy.

Pharmacy Vocabulary

pharmacy	*die Apotheke*
	dee ah poe TAY keh
pharmacist	*der Apotheker/die Apothekerin*
	dare ah poe TAY kuh/
	dee ah poe TAY kuh rin
antibiotic	*das Antibiotikum*
	duss ahn tee bee OH tee koom
antiseptic	*das Antiseptikum*
	duss ahn tee ZEP tee koom
aspirin	*das Aspirin*
	duss ah spee REEN
cough drop	*das Hustenbonbon*
	duss HOOS ten bawn bawn
cough syrup	*der Hustensaft*
	dare HOOS ten zuft
laxative	*das Abführmittel*
	duss AHP fuer mit tell
medicine	*das Medikament*
	duss made ee kah MENT
pill	*die Pille*
	dee PILL eh
prescription	*das Rezept*
	duss ray TSEPT
remedy	*das Heilmittel*
	duss HILE mit tell

tablet (medicine)	*die Tablette*
	dee tah BLETT eh
mild	*mild/leicht*
	millt/lycht
strong	*stark*
	shtahrk

Emergencies and Disasters

You never know what could happen. Just to be on the safe side, here are some words and phrases that would be useful should you ever encounter an emergency.

Emergency Vocabulary

Emergency!	*Notfall!*
	NOTE fuhl
Fire!	*Feuer!*
	FOY uh
Police!	*Polizei!*
	poe lee TSY
Thief!	*Dieb!*
	deep
Watch out!	*Vorsicht!*
	FORE zihcht
accident	*der Unfall*
	dare OON fuhl
attack	*der Angriff*
	dare AHN griff
burglary	*der Einbruch/Diebstahl*
	dare INE brooch/DEEP shtahl

crash	*das Unglück/der Zusammenstoß*
	duss OON glueck/dare tsoo ZAHM en
	shtohs
explosion	*die Explosion*
	dee ex ploe zee OWN
fire	*das Feuer*
	duss FOY uh
fistfight, brawl	*die Schlägerei*
	dee shlay gare EYE
flood	*die Überschwemmung*
	dee ueb uh SHVEMM oong
gunshot	*der Schuss*
	dare shoos
mugging	*der Straßenraub*
	dare SHTRAHS en rowp
rape	*die Vergewaltigung*
	dee fare gheh VULL tee goong
to look for	*suchen*
	ZOO chen
ambulance	*der Krankenwagen*
	dare KRUNK en vah ghen
doctor	*der Arzt/die Ärztin*
	dare ahrtzt/dee AIRTZ tin
firefighter	*der Feuerwehrmann/die Feuerwehrfrau*
	dare FOY uh vare munn/
	dee FOY uh vare frow
help	*die Hilfe*
	dee HILL feh
police officer	*der Polizist/die Polizistin*
	dare poe lee TSIST/dee poe lee TSIS tin

to drown	*ertrinken*
	air TRINK en
to go into labor	*die Wehen bekommen*
	dee VAY en beh KAWM en
to be wounded	*verwundet sein*
	fare VOON det zine

Chapter 12

In Your Community

In the previous chapters, you encountered German phrases that are helpful when traveling, dining out, going shopping, and even finding medical or dental care. This chapter will introduce you to vocabulary that deals with everyday tasks, such as grocery shopping, going to the post office, buying a newspaper, and a variety of other around-town activities.

At the Market

You can do your grocery shopping in Germany by going to the various specialty shops: a bakery, a butcher shop, a dairy store, and so on. Or you can make things more convenient for yourself by doing all your shopping in one place: the supermarket. Whichever you decide to do, the following phrases will come in handy.

Useful Grocery Shopping Terms

grocery store	*das Lebensmittelgeschäft*
	duss LAY bens mit tell gheh sheft
outdoor market	*der Markt*
	dare mahrkt
supermarket	*der Supermarkt*
	dare ZOO puh mahrkt
mall, shopping center	*das Einkaufszentrum*
	duss INE kowfs tsen troom
this one	*dieses*
	DEE zess
that one	*jenes*
	YAY ness
these (ones)	*diese*
	DEE zeh
those (ones)	*jene*
	YAY neh
expensive	*teuer*
	TOY uh
cheap	*billig*
	BILL ik

Fact

The demonstrative pronouns *dieser* and *jener* have to agree with the gender and number of the noun to which they refer. For example, since *Hut* (hat) is masculine, say *dieser Hut* and *jener Hut* (this hat, that hat). With a feminine noun such as *Lampe* (lamp), say *diese Lampe* and *jene Lampe* (this lamp, that lamp). With a neuter noun like *Buch* (book), say *dieses Buch* and *jenes Buch* (this book, that book). Plurals like *Schuhe* (shoes) become *diese Schuhe* and *jene Schuhe* (these shoes, those shoes).

Quantities, Weights, and Measures

It's important to be familiar with the German vocabulary that deals with quantities, in order to make purchases in the amount you want.

How much does it weigh? It weighs . . . kilograms.
Wie viel wiegt es? Es wiegt . . . Kilo.
vee feel veekt es/es veekt . . . KEE loe

Measurement Vocabulary

piece	*ein Stück*
	ine shtueck
box	*eine Schachtel*
	INE eh SHUCH tell
butter dish, can	*eine Dose*
	INE eh DOE zeh

bottle	*eine Flasche*
	INE eh FLUSH eh
jar	*ein Glas*
	ine glahss
gram	*ein Gramm*
	ine grahm
kilogram	*ein Kilogramm*
	ine KEE loe grahm
pound	*ein Pfund*
	ine pfoont
liter	*ein Liter*
	ine LEE tuh
milliliter	*ein Milliliter*
	ine MILL ih lee tuh
can	*eine Büchse*
	INE eh BUEX eh

Useful Measurement Phrases

enough	*genug*
	gheh NOOK
a lot, many	*viel*
	feel
how many, how much	*wie viele/wie viel*
	vee FEE leh/vee feel
more	*mehr*
	mare
less, fewer	*weniger*
	VAY nee guh
a little	*ein bisschen*
	ine BISS chen

191

too much, too many	*zu viel/zu viele*
	tsoo feel/tsoo FEE leh
no more bread	*kein Brot mehr*
	kine brote mare

Alert

When using quantities in German, you don't have to use the word "of" when stating the quantity, such as "a jar of jam." In German, that phrase is *ein Glas Marmalade*. And be sure to review the metric system before arriving in Europe, because inches and gallons aren't used there.

At the Bakery

When you see a sign with the word *Bäkerei* on it, you've found a store that primarily sells bread and rolls. A *Konditorei*, on the other hand, is a store that offers cookies, tarts, cakes, and fancy pastries. It often provides a little seating area where you can snack on a pastry and drink a cup of coffee or glass of wine. The following German vocabulary will be useful when you visit one of these stores.

Bakery Vocabulary

baker	*der Bäcker/die Bäckerin*
	dare BECK uh/dee BECK uh rin
bakery	*die Bäkerei*
	dee BECK uh rye

bread	*das Brot*
	duss brote
rye bread	*das Roggenbrot*
	duss RAW ghen brote
whole-wheat bread	*das Vollkornbrot*
	duss FAWL kohrn brote
a loaf of black bread	*ein Laib Schwarzbrot*
	ine lipe SHVAHRTS brote
roll	*das Brötchen*
	duss BRERT chen
pastry shop	*die Konditorei*
	dee kawn dee toe RYE
doughnut	*der Berliner*
	dare BARE lee nuh
cake	*der Kuchen*
	dare KOOCH en
cookie	*das Plätzchen*
	duss PLETZ chen

At the Post Office

The words *die Post* and *das Postamt* tell you that you are
at the post office.

Postal Vocabulary

post office	*die Post/das Postamt*
	dee pawst/duss PAWST ahmt
mail	*die Post*
	dee pawst
mailbox	*der Briefkasten*
	dare BREEF kuss ten

postage	*das Porto* duss PORE toe
stamp	*die Briefmarke* dee BREEF mahr keh
book of stamps	*das Briefmarkenheft* duss BREEF mahr ken heft
airmail	*die Luftpost* dee LOOFT pawst
zip code	*die Postleitzahl* dee PAWST lite tsahl
change of address	*die Adressenänderung* dee ah DRESS en end uh roong
express mail	*der Eilbrief* dare ILE breef
general delivery	*postlagernd* PAWST lah gairnt
insured	*versichert* fare ZICH airt
receipt	*die Quittung* dee KVIT oong
registered	*eingeschrieben* INE gheh shree ben
postcard	*die Postkarte* dee PAWST kahr teh
special delivery	*die Eilzustellung* dee ILE tsoo shtell oong
address	*die Adresse/Anschrift* dee ah DRESS eh/AHN shrift
envelope	*der Briefumschlag* dare BREEF oom shlahk

letter	*der Brief*
	dare breef
package	*das Paket*
	duss pah KATE
recipient	*der Empfänger/die Empfängerin*
	dare emp FENG uh/
	dee emp FENG uh rin
sender	*der Absender/die Absenderin*
	dare AHP zen duh/dee AHP zen
	duh rin
size	*die Größe*
	dee GRER seh
weight	*das Gewicht*
	duss gheh VICHT
money order	*die Postanweisung*
	dee PAWST ahn vye zoong
postage due	*die Nachgebühr*
	dee NAHCH gheh buer

Alert

If you want to mail letters and postcards when you're out on the street, look for a yellow box. That's the traditional color for the German postal system.

Computers and Cybercafés

If you don't have your computer along on your trip, a good place to check e-mails, print documents, or just surf the net is the cybercafé.

Technology Vocabulary

computer	*der Computer*
	dare kawm PYOO tuh
cybercafé	*das Cybercafé*
	duss SYE buh kah fay
CD-ROM drive	*das CD-ROM-Laufwerk*
	duss tsay day rome LOWF vairk
e-mail	*die E-Mail*
	dee EE mail
e-mail address	*die E-Mail-Adresse*
	dee ee mail ah DRESS eh
file	*die Datei*
	dee dah TYE
hard drive	*das Festplattenlaufwerk*
	duss FEST plutt en lowf vairk
Internet	*das Internet*
	duss IN tuh net
keyboard	*die Tastatur*
	dee tahs tah TOOR
laptop	*der Laptop*
	dare LEP tawp
monitor	*der Monitor/ Bildschirm*
	dare MAWN ee toh/BILT sheerm
mouse	*die Maus*
	dee mouse

mouse button	*die Maustaste*
	dee mouse TUSS teh
per hour	*pro Stunde*
	proe SHTOON deh
printer	*der Drucker*
	dare DROOK uh
software	*die Software*
	dee SAWFT ware
hardware	*die Hardware*
	dee HARD ware
website	*die Website*
	dee WEB site
to download	*herunterladen/downloaden*
	hare OON tuh lah den/DOWN loh den
to receive	*empfangen*
	emp FAHNG en
to send	*senden*
	ZEN den
to click on	*anklicken*
	AHN klick en
to delete	*löschen*
	LER shen

Chapter 13

Miscellaneous German

The categories of vocabulary in this chapter are not interconnected, but they play an important role in the German language. It will be helpful to be familiar with them. You'll encounter words and phrases that deal with weather, physical descriptions, personality, moods, and a little romance.

Weather Words

The weather is always a topic of conversation whether in English or German, so you'll find the following vocabulary useful.

> How's the weather? It is . . .
> *Wie ist das Wetter? Es ist . . .*
> vee ist duss VET tuh ess ist

Weather Vocabulary

hot	*heiß*
	hice
cold	*kalt*
	kult
cool	*kühl*
	kuehl
warm	*warm*
	vahrm
nice	*schön*
	shern
bad	*schlecht*
	shlehcht
humid	*feucht*
	foycht
rainy	*regnerisch*
	RAYG nuh rish
sunny	*sonnig*
	ZAWN ik
cloudy	*bewölkt*
	beh VERLKT

stormy	*stürmisch*
	SHTUER mish
windy	*windig*
	VIN dik
foggy	*neblig*
	NAY blik

The names of the seasons are nouns, so they are always capitalized in German.

Seasons of the Year (*die Jahreszeiten*)

spring	*Frühling/Frühjahr*
	FRUEH ling/FRUEH yahr
summer	*Sommer*
	ZAW muh
autumn	*Herbst*
	hairpst
winter	*Winter*
	VINN tuh

 Fact

> Some weather expressions require the use of a verb instead of an adjective; for example: *Es regnet.* (It's raining.) *Es schneit.* (It's snowing.) *Es donnert.* (It's thundering.) *Es blitzt.* (Lightning is flashing.) *Es gießt in Strömen.* (It's raining cats and dogs.)

Descriptive Data

If you want to describe the new person you're dating or tell the police about a pickpocket you saw, you'll need some descriptive vocabulary.

Descriptive Vocabulary

man	*der Mann*
	dare munn
woman	*die Frau*
	dee frow
boy	*der Junge*
	dare YOONG eh
girl	*das Mädchen*
	duss MATE chen
tall	*groß*
	grohss
short	*klein*
	kline
fat	*dick*
	dick
thin	*dünn*
	duenn
handsome, beautiful	*hübsch*
	huebsh
ugly	*hässlich*
	HESS lich
tan	*sonnengebräunt*
	ZAWN en gheh broynt
pretty	*schön*
	shern

eyes	*die Augen*
	dee OW ghen
hair	*das Haar*
	duss hahr
freckles	*die Sommersprossen*
	dee ZAWM uh shpraws en
dimples	*die Grübchen*
	dee GRUEP chen
wrinkles	*die Falten*
	dee FUL ten

Personality Traits

If you want to describe someone's personality traits rather than physical traits, you need a different kind of vocabulary. Here are some helpful words.

Useful Descriptive Adjectives

athletic	*athletisch/sportlich*
	aht LAY tish/SHPAWRT lich
boring	*langweilig*
	LUNG vye lik
brave	*tapfer*
	TAHPF uh
conceited	*eingebildet*
	INE gheh bill det
cowardly	*feige*
	FYE gheh
forgetful	*vergesslich*
	fare GHESS lich

friendly	*freundlich*
	FROYNT lich
funny	*komisch*
	KOE mish
generous	*großzügig*
	GROHS tsueg ik
hard-working	*fleißig*
	FLY sik
impatient	*ungeduldig*
	OON gheh dool dik
interesting	*interessant*
	in tare eh SAHNT
kind	*nett*
	net
lazy	*faul*
	fowl
likeable	*sympathisch*
	zuem PAH tish
mean	*gemein*
	gheh MINE
naïve	*naiv*
	nah EEF
open-minded	*aufgeschlossen*
	OWF gheh shlaws en
outgoing	*kontaktfreudig*
	kawn TAHKT froy dik
patient	*geduldig*
	gheh DOOL dik
patriotic	*patriotisch*
	pah tree OH tish

playful	*scherzhaft*
	SHAIRTZ huft
reserved	*zurückhaltend*
	tsoo RUEK hult ent
serious	*ernst*
	airnst
shy	*schüchtern*
	SHUECH tuhn
smart	*klug*
	klook
sophisticated	*kultiviert*
	kool tee VEERT
strong	*stark*
	shtahrk
studious	*lerneifrig*
	LAIRN ife rik
stupid	*dumm*
	doom
weak	*schwach*
	shvuhch

Mood Management

Use the following vocabulary to describe someone's mood.

angry	*böse*
	BER zeh
annoying	*ärgerlich*
	AIR guh lich
ashamed	*beschämt*
	beh SHAYMT

calm, quiet	*ruhig*	
	ROO ik	
confident	*zuversichtlich*	
	TSOO fare zihcht lich	
confused	*verwirrt*	
	fare VEERT	
disappointed	*enttäuscht*	
	ent TOYSHT	
embarrassed	*verlegen*	
	fare LAY ghen	
excited	*aufgeregt*	
	OWF gheh raykt	
exhausted	*erschöpft*	
	air SHERPFT	
happy	*froh*	
	froe	
hyperactive	*aufgedreht*	
	OWF gheh drayt	
lonely	*einsam*	
	INE zum	
nervous	*nervös*	
	nare VERSE	
sad	*traurig*	
	TROW rik	
sloppy	*schlampig*	
	SHLUMP ik	
tired	*müde*	
	MUE deh	
worried	*besorgt*	
	beh ZAWRGT	

Alert

Some descriptions in German have to be made by using a verbal expression rather than an adjective; for example: *Ich habe Angst.* (I'm scared.) *Es tut mir Leid.* (I'm sorry.)

The Language of Romance

German is not one of the Romance languages, but still it has a wealth of expressions that have to do with dating, love, and marriage.

I love you, too.
Ich liebe dich auch.
eech LEE beh deech owch

Do you want to marry me?
Willst du mich heiraten?
villst doo meech HYE rah ten

Romantic Vocabulary

to date	*(mit jemandem) ausgehen*
	(mitt YAY mahn dem) OWS gay en
to get engaged	*sich (mit jemandem) verloben*
	zeech (mitt YAY mahn dem) fare LOE ben
to get married	*heiraten*
	HYE rah ten

engagement	*die Verlobung*
	dee fare LOE boong
wedding	*die Hochzeit*
	dee HOECH tsite
wedding anniversary	*der Hochzeitstag*
	dare HOECH tsites tuck
honeymoon	*die Flitterwochen*
	dee FLIT uh vawch en
present	*das Geschenk*
	duss gheh SHENK
flowers	*die Blumen*
	dee BLOO men
candy	*die Süßigkeiten*
	dee ZUESS ik kite en
perfume	*das Parfüm*
	duss pahr FUEM
jewelry	*der Schmuck*
	dare shmook
engagement ring	*der Verlobungsring*
	dare fare LOE boogs ring
wedding ring	*der Ehering*
	dare AYE eh ring
bride	*die Braut*
	dee browt
groom	*der Bräutigam*
	dare BROY tee gahm
husband, spouse	*der Mann/Gatte*
	dare munn/GUT teh
fiancé, fiancée	*der/die Verlobte*
	dare/dee fare LOEP teh

lover	*der/die Geliebte*
	dare/dee gheh LEEP teh
boyfriend	*der Freund*
	dare froynt
wife, spouse	*die Frau/Gattin*
	dee frow/GUT tin
girlfriend	*die Freundin*
	dee FROYN din
acquaintance	*der/die Bekannte*
	dare/dee beh KAHN teh

 Fact

Germans make a clear distinction between a close friend and someone who is a casual friend or acquaintance. Call someone who is dear to you *Freund* or *Freundin*. But someone you just met or who is not very close to you is a *Bekannte*.

Chapter 14

Common German Expressions

In the previous chapters of this book, you encountered vocabulary that was organized by topic or situation. This final chapter is a little different. A series of commonly used German expressions will be presented for their special usage of certain verbs. Some of the expressions are highly idiomatic and can't always be translated literally into English, but in all cases their use will be fully explained.

Espressions with *Es Gibt*

The phrase *es gibt* is used where in English you say "there is" or "there are." *Es gibt* comes from the verb *geben* (to give). However, other special expressions that contain the verb *geben* exist that also don't conform to the general meaning "give."

 Fact

> It is common in all languages to have combinations of words that, when translated into another language, make little or no sense. These are called idioms, and they require special attention.

The Verb *Geben*

Present	Past
ich gebe [GAY beh]	*gab* [gahp]
du gibst [geepst]	*gabst* [gahpst]
er, sie, es gibt [geept]	*gab* [gahp]
wir geben [GAY ben]	*gaben* [GAH ben]
ihr gebt [gaybt]	*gabt* [gahpt]
Sie geben [GAY ben]	*gaben* [GAH ben]
sie geben [GAY ben]	*gaben* [GAH ben]

I don't believe it. (There's no such thing.)
Das gibt es ja gar nicht.
duss geept ess yah gahr nihcht

It happens all the time.
Das gibt es wohl häufiger.
duss geept ess vole HOY fee guh

It wasn't like that back in my day.
Zu meiner Zeit gab es das nicht.
tsoo MINE uh tsite gahp ess duss nihcht

Is there anything else?
Gibt es noch etwas?
geept ess nohch EHT wuss

There'll be rain tomorrow.
Morgen gibt es Regen.
MORE ghen geept ess RAY ghen

There's nothing to eat.
Es gibt nichts zu essen.
ess geebt nihchtz tsoo ESS en

What is there to drink?
Was gibt es zu trinken?
vuss geept ess tsoo TRINK en

What's new?
Was gibt es Neues?
vuss geept ess NOY ess

There's a new movie at the movie theater today.
Im Kino gibt es heute einen neuen Film.
im KEE noe geept ess HOY teh INE en NOY en film

Expressions with *Geben*

to send off to be printed	*zum Druck geben*
	tsoom drook GAY ben
to send out for repairs	*zur Reparatur geben*
	tsoor ray pah rah TOOR GAY ben
to mail	*zur Post geben*
	tsoor pawst GAY ben
to kick	*einen Tritt geben*
	INE en tritt GAY ben
to talk nonsense	*Unsinn von sich geben*
	OON zin fawn zeech GAY ben

 **Alert**

> Although *es gibt* is most often translated as "there is" or "there are," don't confuse that with the adverbs *da* and *dort* which mean "there" as a location.

Expressions with *Machen*

There are a variety of useful expressions that are formed from the verb *machen* (to make). The English translation of some of these special expressions does not make sense if you translate it literally.

Present	Past
ich mache [MAHCH eh]	*machte* [MAHCH teh]
du machst [mahchst]	*machtest* [MAHCH test]
er, sie, es macht [mahcht]	*machte* [MAHCH teh]

wir machen [MAHCH en]	*machten* [MAHCH ten]
ihr macht [mahcht]	*machtet* [MAHCH tet]
Sie machen [MAHCH en]	*machten* [MAHCH ten]
sie machen [MAHCH en]	*machten* [MAHCH ten]

This makes you thirsty.
Das macht Durst.
duss mahcht doorst

This makes you hungry.
Das macht Hunger.
duss mahcht HOONG uh

I take a picture.
Ich mache ein Foto.
eech MAHCH eh ine FOE toe

Make yourself comfortable.
Mach es dir gemütlich.
mahch ess deer gheh MUET lich

What should I do?
Was soll ich nur machen?
vuss zawl eech noor MAHCH en

Expressions with *Machen*

to do one's hair	*sich die Haare machen*
	zeech dee HAH reh MAHCH en
to do one's fingernails	*sich die Fingernägel machen*
	zeech dee FING uhr nay
	ghell MAHCH en
to give a party	*ein Fest machen*
	ine fest MAHCH en

to take a course	*einen Kurs machen*
	INE en koors MAHCH en
to make enemies	*sich Feinde machen*
	zeech FINE deh MAHCH en
to get to work	*sich an die Arbeit machen*
	zeech ahn dee AHR bite
	MAHCH en

 Fact

The verb *machen* is most often translated as "to make." In some expressions it can also be translated as "to do." *Was machst du?* (What are you doing?)

Expressions with *Gehen*

The verb *gehen* means "to go" on foot. But it occurs in other expressions where the meaning is sometimes varied.

The Verb *Gehen*

Present	Past
ich gehe [GAY eh]	*ging* [ging]
du gehst [gayst]	*gingst* [gingst]
er, sie, es geht [gate]	*ging* [ging]
wir gehen [GAY en]	*gingen* [GING en]
ihr geht [gate]	*gingt* [gingt]
Sie gehen [GAY en]	*gingen* [GING en]
sie gehen [GAY en]	*gingen* [GING en]

Yes, that will work.
Ja, das geht.
yah duss gate

This clock is wrong.
Diese Uhr geht falsch.
DEE zeh oor gate fulsh

That will be difficult.
Das wird schwer gehen.
duss vihrd shvare GAY en

How are you (formal)?
Wie geht es Ihnen?
vee gate ess EE nen

I'm fine, thanks.
Es geht mir gut, danke.
ess gate meer goot DUNK eh

He only thinks of money.
Ihm geht es nur um Geld.
eem gate ess noor oom ghelt

Expressions with *Gehen*

to face the street	*nach der Straße gehen*
	nahch dare SHTRAH seh GAY en
to face north	*nach Norden gehen*
	nahch NORE den GAY en
to make a detour	*einen Umweg gehen*
	INE en OOM vake GAY en

to go into the movies	*ins Kino gehen*
	ins KEY no GAY en
to go to bed	*schlafen gehen*
	SHLAH fen GAY en
to go shopping	*einkaufen gehen*
	INE kow fen GAY en

 Alert

> You can use *nach . . . gehen* with any number of expressions that say something "faces" or "looks out on" a place. But *gehen* can also be used with the preposition *zu* and the prefix *hinaus* to achieve a similar meaning.

Expressions with *Lassen*

The basic meaning of *lassen* is "let" or "allow." However, it is frequently used to express that someone "gets" or "has" something done. In addition, there are some useful idiomatic expressions to know.

The Verb *Lassen*

Present	Past
ich lasse [LUSS eh]	*ließ* [lees]
du lässt [lest]	*ließt* [leest]
er, sie, es lässt [lest]	*ließ* [lees]
wir lassen [LUSS en]	*ließen* [LEES en]
ihr lasst [lusst]	*ließt* [leest]

Sie lassen [LUSS en]   *ließen* [LEES en]
sie lassen [LUSS en]   *ließen* [LEES en]

Let the boys enjoy themselves.
Lass den Jungen den Spaß.
luss dane YOONG en dane shpahs

I didn't let the stranger come into my apartment.
Ich ließ den Fremden nicht in meine Wohnung.
eech lees dane FREM den nihcht in MINE eh VOE noong

She gets the car repaired.
Sie lässt den Wagen reparieren.
zee lest dane VAH ghen ray pah REE ren

I got my suit dry-cleaned.
Ich ließ mir den Anzug reinigen.
eech lees meer dane AHN tsook RINE ih gen

Expressions with *Lassen*

to run water in the bathtub	*Wasser in die Wanne laufen lassen*
	VUSS uh in dee VUNN eh LOW fen LUSS en
to send one's regards	*grüßen lassen*
	GRUE sen LUSS en
to let know	*wissen lassen*
	VISS en LUSS en
to leave in peace	*in Frieden lassen*
	in FREE den LUSS en
to leave alone	*allein lassen*
	ah LINE LUSS en

Lassen is often used in an impersonal expression that means "it can be . . . " In the present and past tenses, it is stated as *es lässt sich* and *es ließ sich*.

The door can't be opened.
Die Tür lässt sich nicht öffnen.
dee tuer lest zeech nihcht ERF nen

That can be done.
Das lässt sich machen.
duss lest zeech MAHCH en

It couldn't be denied.
Es ließ sich nicht verleugnen.
ess lees zeech nihcht fare LOYG nen

That couldn't be proved.
Das ließ sich nicht beweisen.
duss lees zeech nihcht beh VIZE en

Expressions with *Tun*

The verb *tun* means "to do" and has a variety of uses with that meaning. However, it appears in special expressions where that meaning is often changed.

The Verb *Tun*

Present	Past
ich tue [TOO eh]	*tat* [taht]
du tust [toost]	*tatst* [tahtst]
er, sie, es tut [toot]	*tat* [taht]
wir tun [toon]	*taten* [TAHT en]

ihr tut [toot]	*tatet* [TAHT et]
Sie tun [toon]	*taten* [TAHT en]
sie tun [toon]	*taten* [TAHT en]

What are you doing here?
Was tun Sie hier?
vuss toon zee heer

What should I do?
Was soll ich tun?
vuss zawl eech toon

There's nothing you can do about it.
Dagegen kannst du nichts tun.
dah GAY ghen kahnst doo nihchst toon

Go on!
Tu's doch!
toose dawch

I'm busy.
Ich habe zu tun.
eech HAH beh tsoo toon

Don't do this to me!
Tu mir das nicht an!
too meer duss nihcht ahn

She's got a heart problem.
Sie hat es mit dem Herzen zu tun.
zee haht ess mitt dame HARE tsen tsoo toon

Expressions with *Tun*

to have its effect	*seine Wirkung tun*
	ZINE eh VIRK oong toon
to do a favor	*einen Gefallen tun*
	INE en gheh FULL en toon
to put water in the pot	*Wasser in den Topf tun*
	VUSS uh in dane tawpf toon
to act as if . . .	*tun, als ob . . .*
	toon ahls awp

When *nicht* is in a sentence with a prepositional phrase, there is a tendency to place *nicht* in front of the prepositional phrase: *Ich komme nicht aus Deutschland.* (I don't come from Germany.) *Heute gehen die Kinder nicht ins Kino.* (The children aren't going to the movies today.)

The Modal Auxiliaries

The modal auxiliaries have an important function in the German language. They describe a person's attitude or obligation regarding an activity. The modals are: *dürfen* (may, be allowed), *können* (can, to be able to), *müssen* (must, to have to), *sollen* (should, ought to), and *wollen* (to want to).

Their present and past tense conjugations are:

The Verb *Dürfen*

Present	Past
ich darf [dahrf]	*durfte* [DOORF teh]
du darfst [dahrfst]	*durftest* [DOORF test]
er, sie, es darf [dahrf]	*durfte* [DOORF teh]

wir dürfen [DUERF en]   *durften* [DOORF ten]
ihr dürft [duerft]   *durftet* [DOORF tet]
Sie dürfen [DUERF en]   *durften* [DOORF ten]
sie dürfen [DUERF en]   *durften* [DOORF ten]

The Verb *Können*

Present	Past
ich kann [kahn]	*konnte* [KAWN teh]
du kannst [kahnst]	*konntest* [KAWN test]
er, sie, es kann [kahn]	*konnte* [KAWN teh]
wir können [KERN en]	*konnten* [KAWN ten]
ihr könnt [kernt]	*konntet* [KAWN tet]
Sie können [KERN en]	*konnten* [KAWN ten]
sie können [KERN en]	*konnten* [KAWN ten]

The Verb *Müssen*

Present	Past
ich muss [moos]	*musste* [MOOS teh]
du musst [moosst]	*musstest* [MOOS test]
er, sie, es muss [moos]	*musste* [MOOS teh]
wir müssen [MUESS en]	*mussten* [MOOS ten]
ihr müsst [muesst]	*musstet* [MOOS tet]
Sie müssen [MUESS en]	*mussten* [MOOS ten]
sie müssen [MUESS en]	*mussten* [MOOS ten]

The Verb *Sollen*

Present	Past
ich soll [zawl]	*sollte* [ZAWL teh]
du sollst [zawlst]	*solltest* [ZAWL test]
er, sie, es soll [zawl]	*sollte* [ZAWL teh]
wir sollen [ZAWL en]	*sollten* [ZAWL ten]
ihr sollt [zawlt]	*solltet* [ZAWL tet]
Sie sollen [ZAWL en]	*sollten* [ZAWL ten]
sie sollen [ZAWL en]	*sollten* [ZAWL ten]

The Verb *Wollen*

Present	Past
ich will [vill]	*wollte* [VAWL teh]
du willst [villst]	*wolltest* [VAWL test]
er, sie, es will [vill]	*wollte* [VAWL teh]
wir wollen [VAWL en]	*wollten* [VAWL ten]
ihr wollt [vawlt]	*wolltet* [VAWL tet]
Sie wollen [VAWL en]	*wollten* [VAWL ten]
sie wollen [VAWL en]	*wollten* [VAWL ten]

Using Modal Auxiliaries

The modal auxiliaries are used together with another verb—an infinitive, for example *mitkommen*.

Common Expressions

May I come along?	*Darf ich mitkommen?*
	dahrf eech MIT kaw men
Can they come along?	*Können sie mitkommen?*
	KERN en zee MIT kaw men

Do I have to come along? *Muss ich mitkommen?*
moos eech MIT kaw men
Should he come along? *Soll er mitkommen?*
zawl air MIT kaw men
Do you want to come along? *Wollen Sie mikommen?*
VAWL en zee MIT kaw men

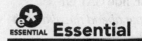

ESSENTIAL Essential

> Notice that the infinitive in sentences with modals appears at the end of the sentence. Any number of infinitives can be used with each of the modal auxiliaries.

We have to . . .
Wir müssen . . .
veer MUESS en

Wir müssen . . .

. . . drive to the city	. . . *in die Stadt fahren*
	in dee shtuht FAH ren
. . . go shopping	. . . *einkaufen gehen*
	INE kow fen GAY en
. . . find the money	. . . *das Geld finden*
	duss ghelt FIN den
. . . buy two airline tickets	. . . *zwei Flugtickets kaufen*
	tsvy FLOOK tick ets KOW fen

Do you want . . .
Willst du . . .
villst doo

Willst du . . .

. . . to go to the movies?	. . . *ins Kino gehen?* Ins KEE noe GAY en
. . . to go out for Mexican this evening?	. . . *heute abend mexikanisch essen?* HOY teh AH bent mex ee KAH nish ESS en

I can't . . .
Ich kann nicht . . .
eech kahn nihcht

Ich kann nicht . . .

. . . understand	. . . *verstehen* fare SHTAY en
. . . sleep	. . . *schlafen* SHLAH fen
. . . go to the theater	. . . *ins Theater gehen* ins tay AH tuh GAY en

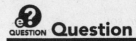

Question

How do I use the modal auxiliaries in the future tense?
As with all infinitives in future tense sentences, the modal auxiliary infinitive appears at the end of the sentence. But since modals are used with other infinitives, the future tense sentence will have two infinitives at the end. Present Tense: *Er kann es nicht verstehen.* (He can't understand it.) Future Tense: *Er wird es nicht verstehen können.* (He won't be able to understand it.)

The Special Case of *Haben*

A very important phrase is formed with the subjunctive of *haben* (to have). Its conjugational forms are: *ich hätte, du hättest, er/sie/es hätte, wir hätten, ihr hättet, Sie hätten, sie hätten.* It is used together with *sollen* to express regret at someone's actions: *Das hättest du nicht tun sollen.* (You shouldn't have done that.)

You shouldn't have . . .
Das hätten Sie nicht . . . sollen
duss HETT en zee nihcht . . . zawlen

Das hätten Sie nicht . . .

. . . said that	. . . *sagen sollen*
	ZAH ghen ZAWL en
. . . bought that	. . . *kaufen sollen*
	KOW fen ZAWL en

225

... written that	... *schreiben sollen*
	SHRY ben ZAWL en
... ordered that	... *bestellen sollen*
	beh SHTELL en ZAWL en
... asked that	... *fragen sollen*
	FRAH ghen ZAWL en
... broken that	... *kaputt machen sollen*
	kah POOT MAHCH en ZAWL en
... lost that	... *verlieren sollen*
	fare LEER en ZAWL en

Alert

This kind of special phrase is really quite easy to use. Just don't forget that the sentence ends with two infinitives side by side: *Das hätte ich nicht essen sollen.* (I shouldn't have eaten that.)

Special Phrases and Word Order

In general, there are not many complications with German word order. One exception is the placement of an infinitive at the end of a sentence that has a modal auxiliary. Many conjunctions also signal a word order change.

Using *Dass* and *Ob*

The conjunctions *dass* (that) and *ob* (whether/if) require the conjugated verb in the clause that follows them to be the last element. These conjunctions are used frequently with an important verb: *wissen* (to know). Here are this verb's present and past tense conjugations.

The Verb *Wissen*

Present	Past
ich weiß [vice]	*wusste* [VOOS teh]
du weißt [vysst]	*wusstest* [VOOS test]
er, sie, es weiß [vice]	*wusste* [VOOS teh]
wir wissen [VISS en]	*wussten* [VOOS ten]
ihr wisst [visst]	*wusstet* [VOOS tet]
Sie wissen [VISS en]	*wussten* [VOOS ten]
sie wissen [VISS en]	*wussten* [VOOS ten]

Alert

Don't confuse *wissen* and *kennen*. They both mean "to know." However, *wissen* means having knowledge and *kennen* means being acquainted with someone; for example: *Ich weiß, wo er wohnt.* (I know where he lives.) *Ich kenne die junge Frau.* (I know the young woman.)

I know.
Ich weiß.
Eech vice

I don't know.
Ich weiß (es) nicht.
Ecch vice ess nihcht

As far as I know.
Soviel ich weiß.
Zoe feel eech vice

You always know better.
Sie wissen immer alles besser.
Zee VISS en IM muh ULL ess BESS uh

How should a person know that?
Woher soll man das wissen?
VOE hare zawl munn duss VISS en

You never know!
Man kann nie wissen!
Munn kahn nee VISS en

I don't know anything about it.
Ich weiß von nichts.
Eech vice fawn nihchts

Wissen

to know about	*wissen von*
	VISS en fawn
to know how to behave	*sich zu benehmen wissen*
	zeech tsoo beh NAME en VISS en

When *wissen* is used with the conjunctions *dass* and *ob*, the conjugated verb appears at the end of the sentence.

I know that . . .
Ich weiß, dass . . .
eech vice duss

Ich weiß, dass . . .

. . . the hotel isn't far from here
. . . *das Hotel nicht weit von hier entfernt ist*
duss HOE tell nihcht vite fawn heer ent FAIRNT ist

. . . his brother is well again
. . . *sein Bruder wieder gesund ist*
zine BROO duh VEE duh gheh ZOONT ist

. . . I need more money
. . . *ich mehr Geld brauche*
eech mare ghelt BROW cheh

. . . she bought a blouse
. . . *sie eine Bluse kaufte*
zee INE eh BLOO zeh KOWF teh

Do you know whether (if) . . .
Wissen Sie, ob . . .
VISS en zee awp

Wissen Sie, ob . . .

. . . the inn is still open?
. . . *der Gasthof noch offen ist?*
Dare GAHST hofe nawch AW fen ist

. . . this street goes to city hall?
. . . *diese Straße zum Rathaus führt?*
DEEZ eh SHTRAH seh tsoom RAHT house fuert

. . . they have my luggage?
. . . *sie mein Gepäck haben?*
Zee mine gheh PECK HAH ben

. . . service is included?
. . . *die Bedienung inbegriffen ist?*
Dee beh DEEN oong in beh GRIFF en ist

You can even use interrogative words like *wann*, *wo*, and *wie* as conjunctions that require the same word order.

Do you know when the next train will arrive?
Weißt du, wann der nächste Zug kommt?
Vysst doo vunn dare NAYX teh tsook kawmt

I don't know where Mr. Keller lives.
Ich weiß nicht, wo Herr Keller wohnt.
Ecch vice nihcht voe hare KELL uh voent

Do you know how you get to the airport?
Wissen Sie, wie man zum Flughafen kommt?
VISS en zee vee munn tsoom FLOOK hah fen kawmt

ⓔ❓ QUESTION **Question**

How do I know when a verb will be the last element in a clause?
All conjunctions like *dass* and *ob* and interrogatives like *wann* and *wo* require the verb to be the last element in a clause. There are four exceptions to that rule: *aber* (but), *denn* (because), *oder* (or), and *und* (and).

Imperatives

Because there are three forms of "you" in German, there are three forms of the commands: one for *du*, one for *ihr*, and one for *Sie*.

Commands with *Du*

Most second person singular commands (*du*) are formed by dropping the *–en* ending from an infinitive. This is the imperative that is used with family members, friends, or children.

Infinitive	Imperative	English
kommen	*Komm!*	Come!
singen	*Sing!*	Sing!
fahren	*Fahr schneller!*	Drive faster!
machen	*Mach schnell!*	Hurry up!
spielen	*Spiel im Garten.*	Play in the garden.

Commands with *Ihr*

The pronoun *ihr* is the informal plural of *du*. Its imperative form is usually identical to its present tense conjugation.

Infinitive	Imperative	English
lachen	*Lacht nicht!*	Don't laugh!
singen	*Singt!*	Sing!
sprechen	*Sprecht Deutsch!*	Speak German!
bleiben	*Bleibt zu Hause!*	Stay at home!
downloaden	*Downloadet neue Software!*	Download new software!

Commands with *Sie*

The *Sie* form of the imperative is the formal form. In most cases, use the infinitive and place the pronoun *Sie* after it, and you will have the command form.

Infinitive	Imperative	English
sich setzen	*Setzen Sie sich!*	Sit down!
helfen	*Helfen Sie mir!*	Help me!
verkaufen	*Verkaufen Sie den Wagen.*	Sell the car.
aufhören	*Hören Sie auf!*	Stop that!
sein	*Seien Sie nicht böse!*	Don't be angry!

Fact

In public places where announcements are made, you will often hear an imperative given in the form of an infinitive. If you use this form with a person you're speaking with, it will sound a bit abrupt. It's used primarily to give information to large groups; for example: *Zurückbleiben!* (Stand back!) *Nicht Rauchen!* (No smoking!)

Appendix A

German–English Dictionary

The gender and number of the nouns listed here are indicated by m. for masculine, f. for feminine, n. for neuter, sing. for singular, and pl. for plural. Both German and English verbs are provided as infinitives.

Abend m.	evening
Abendbrot n.	dinner, supper
Abendessen n.	dinner, supper
aber	but
abfertigen	to check in
Abfertigungsschalter m.	check-in counter
Abflug m.	departure (plane)
Abführmittel n.	laxative
abgeben	to hand in
abheben	to answer (the phone); withdraw (from an account)
Abitur n.	high-school diploma, school-leaving exam
abnehmen	to take off, take from
Abreise f.	departure
abschalten	to turn off
Absender m.	sender
abstrakt	abstract
Abszess m.	abscess
ach	oh, alas
acht	eight
achtzehn	eighteen
achtzig	eighty
Adresse f.	address
Affe m.	ape, monkey
Afrikaner m., *Afrikanerin* f.	African
Ägypter m., *Ägypterin* f.	Egyptian
Aktenschrank m.	filing cabinet
Aktentasche f.	briefcase
aktiv	active
Akzent m.	accent
alle	all, everyone
allein	alone
Allergie f.	allergy
allergisch	allergic
alles	everything
als ob	as if
alt	old
Amerika n.	America
Amerikaner m., *Amerikanerin* f.	American
Änderung f.	change
angeln	to fish
Angestellte m./f.	employee
Angriff m.	attack
Angst haben	to be afraid

Anhänger m.	pendant
anklicken	to click on
Ankunft f.	arrival
Anrufbeantworter m.	answering machine
anrufen	to call (phone)
anschalten	to turn on
Anschrift f.	mailing address
ansehen (sich)	to look at, watch
Ansichtskarte f.	picture postcard
Anstecknadel f.	pin (decorative)
Antibiotikum n.	antibiotic
anziehen (sich)	to dress (oneself)
Anzug m.	suit
Apfel m.	apple
Apfelsine f.	orange
Apotheke f.	pharmacy, drugstore
Apotheker m., *Apothekerin* f.	pharmacist
Apparat m.	apparatus, appliance
Appetit m.	appetite
Aprikose f.	apricot
April m.	April
Arbeit f.	work, job
arbeitslos	jobless
ärgerlich	annoyed, annoying
Arm m.	arm
Armband n.	bracelet
Arthritis f.	arthritis
Artischocke f.	artichoke
Artist m., *Artistin* f.	artist
Arzt m., *Ärztin* f.	doctor, physician
Aspirin n.	aspirin
Asthmatiker m.	asthmatic (person)
asthmatisch	asthmatic
athletisch	athletic
attraktiv	attractive
auch	also, too
auf	on
auf Wiederhören	goodbye (on phone)
auf Wiedersehen	goodbye
Aufführung f.	performance
aufgeben	to give up; check in (luggage)
aufgedreht	hyperactive
aufgeregt	excited
aufgeschlossen	open-minded
aufhängen	to hang up (phone)

aufhören	to stop, cease
aufmachen	to open
Auge n.	eye
Augenzahn m.	eyetooth
August m.	August
aus	out, from
ausgeben	to spend (money)
ausspülen	to rinse out
Ausweis m.	identification
ausziehen (sich)	to undress (oneself)
Auto n.	car
Autobahn f.	superhighway, expressway
Automatikgetriebe n.	automatic transmission
Automobil n.	automobile
Baby n.	baby
Backe f.	cheek
Backenzahn m.	molar
Bäcker m., *Bäckerin* f.	baker
Bäckerei f.	bakery
Badeanzug m.	bathing suit, swimsuit
Badewanne f.	bathtub
Bahnhof m.	train station
Bahnsteig m.	train platform
Balkon m.	balcony
Ballett n.	ballet
Banane f.	banana
Band n.	ribbon
Bank f.	bank
bar	in cash
Bär m.	bear
Bargeld n.	cash
Baseball m.	baseball
Basketball m.	basketball
Beamte m., *Beamtin*, f.	civil servant, official
bedeuten	to mean
Bedienung f.	service; call to the waiter
bei	by, at
Bein n.	leg
Bekannte m./f.	acquaintance
Bekleidungsgeschäft n.	clothing store
belegt	no vacancy
benehmen (sich)	to behave
Benzin n.	gasoline
Berliner m.	doughnut
Beruf m.	occupation

beschämt	ashamed
beschleunigen	to accelerate
besetzt	busy, engaged (phone)
besorgt	worried
bestätigt	certified
bestellen	to order
besuchen	to visit
Betäubung f.	anesthesia
Betrag m.	total, amount
Bett n.	bed
beweisen	to prove
bewerben (sich)	to apply for
bezahlen	to pay for
BH m.	bra
Bier n.	beer
Bikini m.	bikini
Bildschirm m.	monitor, screen
billig	cheap
Billion f.	trillion
Birne f.	pear
bis	until
bisschen (ein)	a little, a bit
bitte	please
blau	blue
Blaubeere f.	blueberry
bleiben	to remain, stay
Bleichmittel n.	bleach
Bleistift m.	pencil
blind	blind
Blinker m.	turn signal
blitzen	to flash (lightning)
Blume f.	flower
Blumenkohl m.	cauliflower
Bluse f.	blouse
Blutdruck m.	blood pressure
bluten	to bleed
Bohne f.	bean
Boot n.	boat
Bordkarte f.	boarding pass
böse	angry, mad
Boxershorts pl.	boxer shorts
Brasilianer m.	Brazilian
brauchen	to need
braun	brown
Braut f.	bride

Bräutigam m.	groom
brechen	to break
Bremse f.	brake
Bremslicht n.	brake light
Brief m.	letter
Briefkasten m.	mailbox
Briefmarke f.	postage stamp
Briefmarkenheft n.	book of stamps
Brieftasche f.	wallet
Briefumschlag m.	envelope
Brille f.	eyeglasses
Brombeere f.	blackberry
Brosche f.	broach
Brot n.	bread
Brötchen n.	roll
Bruder m.	brother
Brunnen m.	well, fountain
Brust f.	chest
Buch n.	book
Büchse f.	can
Büroklammer f.	paper clip
bürsten	to brush
Büstenhalter m.	brassiere
bummeln	to stroll
Bus m.	bus
Busbahnhof m.	bus station
Bushaltestelle f.	bus stop
Butter f.	butter
Buttermilch f.	buttermilk
CD-ROM-Laufwerk n.	CD-ROM drive
Chance f.	chance
Chef m., *Chefin* f.	boss
chemische Reinigung f.	dry cleaner
Cocktail m.	cocktail
Computer m.	computer
Cousin m., *Cousine* f.	cousin
Cybercafé n.	cybercafé
da	there
dagegen	against it
damit	with it
danken	to thank
Darlehen n.	loan
das	the (n.), that
dass	that
Datei f.	file

238

Dauerwelle f.	permanent, perm
Daumen m.	thumb
dein	your (*du*)
demokratisch	democratic
denn	because
der	the (m.)
deutsch	German
Deutsche m./f.	German (person)
Deutschland n.	Germany
Dezember m.	December
Diabetiker m., *Diabetikerin* f.	diabetic (person)
diabetisch	diabetic
Diät f.	diet
dick	fat, thick
die	the (f.)
Dieb m.	thief
Diebstahl m.	theft
Dienstag m.	Tuesday
Dienstmädchen n.	maid
dieser, diese, dieses	this
Diplomat m., *Diplomatin* f.	diplomat
doch	but, still
Doktorgrad m.	doctorate
donnern	to thunder
Donnerstag m.	Thursday
Doppelbett n.	double bed
dort	there
dort drüben	over there
Dose f.	butter dish, can, box
drei	three
dreißig	thirty
dreizehn	thirteen
Drogerie f.	drugstore
Druck m.	print, printing
Drucker m.	printer
du	you (sing., informal)
dünn	thin
dürfen	may, to be allowed
dumm	stupid
dunkelblau	dark blue
durch	through
Durchfall m.	diarrhea
durchgebraten	well done (meat)
durchspülen	to rinse
Durst m.	thirst

Dusche f.	shower
duschen (sich)	to take a shower
duzen	to say *du* to (address informally)
Eckzahn m.	canine tooth
Economywagen m.	economy car
effektiv	effective
Ehering m.	wedding ring
Ei n.	egg
Eilbrief m.	express letter
Eilzustellung f.	express delivery
ein, eine	a, an
einander	one another, each other
Einbahnstraße f.	one-way street
einbiegen	to turn (automobile)
Einbruch m.	burglary, break-in
eingebildet	conceited
eingeschrieben	registered
einkaufen	to shop
Einkaufszentrum n.	mall, shopping center
einlösen	to cash (in)
einmal	once
eins	one
einsam	lonely
Einsamkeit f.	loneliness
einstellen	to employ
einzahlen	to deposit (money)
Eis n.	ice; ice cream
Elefant m.	elephant
Elektriker m., *Elektrikerin* f.	electrician
elf	eleven
Ellbogen m.	elbow
E-Mail f.	e-mail
E-Mail-Adresse f.	e-mail address
empfangen	to receive
Empfänger m., *Empfängerin* f.	recipient, addressee
Empfangschef m., *Empfangsdame* f.	receptionist (hotel)
England n.	England
Engländer m., *Engländerin* f.	Englishman, Englishwoman
englisch	English
englisch gebraten	rare (meat)
Enkel m., *Enkelin* f.	grandchild
entfernt	remote, (away) from
entlassen	to fire, dismiss
Entschuldigung f.	excuse
enttäuscht	disappointed

er	he, it (m.)
erbrechen (sich)	to throw up
Erbsen pl.	peas
Erdbeere f.	strawberry
Erdgeschoss n.	first gloor (U.S.), ground floor (UK)
Erdnuss f.	peanut
Erfrierungen pl.	frostbite
erkälten (sich)	to catch a cold
Erkältung f.	cold (illness)
erklären	to declare; explain
ernst	serious
erschöpft	exhausted
ersetzen	to replace
Ertrag m.	gain, yield (financial)
ertrinken	to drown
es	it
es gibt	there is/are
es lässt sich	it can be
essen	to eat
Esszimmer n.	dining room
etwas	something
euer	your *(ihr)*
Europäer m., *Europäerin* f.	European
Examen n.	exam
Explosion f.	explosion
extrahieren	to extract
Fach n.	subject (school).
fahren (mit)	to drive, go (by)
Fahrer m., *Fahrerin* f.	driver
Fahrrad n.	bicycle
Fahrstuhl m.	elevator
Fahrt f.	drive, trip
fair	fair
Fakultät f.	department (school)
fallen	to fall
falsch	false, wrong
Falten pl.	wrinkles
Familie f.	family
Familienname m.	surname
Farbe f.	color
färben	to color, dye
faul	lazy
Fausthandschuhe pl.	mittens
Faxgerät n.	fax machine
Februar m.	February

feige	cowardly
Feind m.	enemy
Feld n.	field
Fenster n.	window
Ferngespräch n.	long-distance call
Fernlicht n.	high beams
Fernsehapparat m.	television set
fernsehen	to watch television
Fernsehsendung f.	television program
Fest n.	celebration
Festplattenlaufwerk n.	hard drive
Fett n.	fat
feucht	humid
Feuer n.	fire
Feuerwehrmann m., *Feuerwehrfrau* f.	firefighter
Fieber n.	fever
Film m.	film, movie
Filz m.	felt
finden	to find
Finger m.	finger
Fingernagel m.	fingernail
Firma f.	company
Fisch m.	fish
fischen	to fish
Fischgeschäft n.	fish market
Flasche f.	bottle
Fleisch n.	meat
Fleischer m., *Fleischerin* f.	butcher
Fleischerei f.	butcher shop
fleißig	diligent, hard-working
Fliege f.	bow tie; fly
fliegen	to fly
Flitterwochen pl.	honeymoon
Floppy Disk f.	floppy disk
Flöte f.	flute
Flug m.	flight
Fluggast m.	airline passenger
Fluggesellschaft f.	airline
Flughafen m.	airport
Flugsteig m.	gate (airport)
Flugticket n.	airline ticket
Flugzeug n.	airplane
Flur m.	hallway
fönen	to blow-dry
Foto n.	photo

fragen	to ask
Franzose m., *Französin* f.	Frenchman, Frenchwoman
Frau f.	woman, wife
Frauenkleidung f.	women's clothing
Freitag m.	Friday
Fremde m./f.	stranger
freuen (sich)	to be glad, happy
Freund m., *Freundin* f.	friend, boyfriend/girlfriend
freundlich	kind, friendly
freundschaftlich	friendly
Frieden m.	peace
frisch	fresh
Frischkäse m.	cream cheese
Friseur m.	barber, hair stylist
Frisur f.	hairdo
froh	happy
Frosch m.	frog
früh	early
Frühling m.	spring
Frühstück n.	breakfast
führen	to lead
Füller m.	(fountain) pen
fünf	five
fünfzehn	fifteen
fünfzig	fifty
für	for
Fuß m.	foot
Fußball m.	soccer
Fußgelenk n.	ankle
Gabel f.	fork
gar	at all
Garage f.	garage
Garten m.	garden
Gartenarbeit f.	gardening
Gärtner m., *Gartnerin* f.	gardner
gärtnern	to garden
Gas n.	gas
Gaspedal n.	gas pedal
Gasse f.	lane
Gasthof m.	inn
Gatte m., *Gattin* f.	spouse
geben	to give
Gebühr f.	fee, toll
Gedeck n.	fixed menu
geduldig	patient

Gefallen m.	favor
Geflügel n.	poultry
gegen	against
gehen	to go (on foot)
Geige f.	violin
gelb	yellow
Geld n.	money
Geldautomat m.	ATM
Geldschein m.	bill, paper money
Geldwechsel m.	currency exchange
Geliebte m./f.	lover
gemein	mean, nasty
gemütlich	cozy, comfortable
Generaldirektor m.	CEO
genug	enough
Gepäck n.	baggage, luggage
Gepäckausgabe f.	baggage claim
geradeaus	straight ahead
gern	gladly
Geschäft n.	store
Geschäftskarte f.	business card
geschehen	to happen
Geschenk n.	present, gift
Geschwindigkeitsbeschränkung f.	speed limit
Gesicht n.	face
gesund	healthy
Gesundheit f.	health; bless you (after a sneeze)
Getränk n.	drink, beverage
Gewicht n.	weight
Gewitter n.	storm
gießen	to pour
Girokonto n.	checking account
Gitarre f.	guitar
Glas n.	glass, jar
gleich	equal, same
Golf n.	golf
Grab n.	grave
Gramm n.	gram
grau	gray
Grippe f.	flu
groß	big, large, tall
Größe f.	size
Großmutter f.	grandmother
Großvater m.	grandfather
großzügig	generous

German	English
Grübchen n.	dimple
grün	green
grüßen	to greet
Gürtel m.	belt
Gurke f.	cucumber
gut	good, well
Gymnasium n.	high school
Haar n.	hair
Haarspange f.	barrette
haben	to have
habilitieren	to habilitate, qualify as a professor
Hähnchen n.	chicken
halb	half
halb durchgebraten	medium rare/well (meat)
hallo	hi
Hals m.	neck
Halskette f.	necklace
Halstuch n.	neckerchief, scarf
Hämorrhoiden pl.	hemorrhoids
Hand f.	hand
Handgelenk n.	wrist
Handgepäck n.	carry-on luggage
Handschuhe pl.	gloves
Handtasche f.	handbag, purse
Handtuch n.	towel
Handy n.	cell phone
Hardware f.	hardware (computer)
hart	hard
hässlich	ugly
häufig	frequent
Hauptfach n.	major, main subject (academic)
Hauptgericht n.	main course
Haus n.	house
Hausaufgaben f.	homework
Haustier n.	pet
Heft n.	notebook
Hefter m.	stapler
Heftklammer f.	staple
Heidelbeere f.	blueberry
Heilmittel n.	remedy
Heimweh n.	homesickness
heiraten	to marry
heiß	hot
heißen	to be called
heizen	to heat

helfen	to help
hellblau	light blue
Hemd n.	shirt
Herbst m.	autumn
Hering m.	herring
Herr m.	Mr., sir
herunterladen	to download
Herz n.	heart
Heuschnupfen m.	hay fever
heute	today
Hilfe f.	help, aid
Himbeere f.	raspberry
hinken	to limp
hinlegen (sich)	to lie down
hinsetzen (sich)	to sit down
hinter	behind, in back of
hinterlassen	to leave (behind)
Hin- und Rückflugkarte f.	round-trip airline ticket
historisch	historic
Hitze f.	heat
hoch	high
hochhackig Schuhe pl.	high-heeled shoes
Hochschule f.	higher education institute
Hochstuhl m.	highchair
Hochzeit f.	wedding
Hochzeitstag m.	wedding anniversary
Hockey n.	hockey
holen	to get, fetch
hören	to hear
Hörer m.	receiver (phone)
Hose f.	pants
Hotel n.	hotel
hübsch	beautiful, handsome
Huhn n.	chicken
Hummer m.	lobster
hundert	hundred
Hunger m.	hunger
Hustenbonbon n.	cough drop
Hustensaft m.	cough syrup
Hut m.	hat
ich	I
ihr	you (pl., informal)
ihr	her, their
immatrikulieren	to matriculate
immer	always

inbegriffen	included
Inder m., *Inderin* f.	Indian (East)
Industrie f.	industry
infiziert	infected
Ingenieur m., *Ingenieurin* f.	engineer
Inhalationsapparat m.	inhaler
Injektion f.	injection
innovativ	innovative
interessant	interesting
interessieren (sich)	to interest
Internet n.	Internet
Italiener m., *Italienerin* f.	Italian
ja	yes
Jacke f.	jacket
Jagd f.	hunt
jagen	to hunt
Januar m.	January
Japaner m., *Japanerin* f.	Japanese
Jeans pl.	jeans
jeder, jede, jedes	each
jemand	someone
jener, jene, jenes	that
Job m.	job
Jod n.	iodine
joggen	to jog
Joghurt m.	yogurt
Juli m.	July
Junge m.	boy
Juni m.	June
Kabrio n.	convertible
Kaffee m.	coffee
Kakao m.	cocoa
Kalb n.	calf
Kalbfleisch n.	veal
kalt	cold (temperature)
Kanadier m., *Kanadierin* f.	Canadian
Kapitalist m.	capitalist
kaputt	broken
Kapuzenpulli m.	hoodie
Karotte f.	carrot
Karten pl.	cards (playing)
Kartoffel f.	potato
Käse m.	cheese
kaufen	to buy
Kaufhaus n.	department store

kein	no, not a, not any
Keller m.	basement, cellar
Kellner m., *Kellnerin* f.	waiter, server
kennen	to know, be acquainted
kennen lernen	to become acquainted
Kette f.	chain
Kiefer m.	jaw
Kilo n.	kilogram
Kilogramm n.	kilogram
Kilometer m.	kilometer
Kind n.	child
Kindergarten m.	kindergarten
Kino n.	movie theater
Kirche f.	church
Kirsche f.	cherry
Kissen n.	pillow
Klasse f.	class, grade (year in school)
Klassenzimmer n.	classroom
Klavier n.	piano
Kleid n.	dress
Kleidergröße f.	dress size, clothing size
Kleiderschrank m.	wardrobe
klein	small, little
Kleingeld n.	change (money)
Klempner m., *Klempnerin* f.	plumber
Klimaanlage f.	air conditioning
klingeln	to ring
klug	smart, clever
Knabe m.	lad, boy
Knecht m.	farmhand
Knie n.	knee
Koch m., *Köchin* f.	cook
kochen	to cook
komisch	funny
kommen	to come
kommunistisch	communist
Kompaktwagen m.	compact car
Konditorei f.	pastry shop
Konferenz f.	conference
können	can, to be able to
kontaktfreudig	outgoing, sociable
Kontoauszug m.	bank statement
Kontostand m.	bank balance
Konzert n.	concert
Kopf m.	head

Kopfsalat m.	lettuce
Kopfschmerzen pl.	headache
Kopiergerät n.	copy machine
Korbball m.	basketball
korrekt	correct
Korridor m.	corridor
kosten	to cost
krank	sick
Krankenhaus n.	hospital
Krankenpfleger m., *Krankenschwester* f.	nurse
Krankenwagen m.	ambulance
Krawattenhalter m.	tie clip
Kreditkarte f.	credit card
Kreide f.	chalk
kritisch	critical
Kuchen m.	cake
Küche f.	kitchen
kühl	cool
Künstler m., *Künstlerin* f.	artist
küssen	to kiss
Kuh f.	cow
kultiviert	sophisticated
Kummerbund m.	cummerbund
Kursus m.	course (school)
kurz	short (time, length, distance)
lachen	to laugh
Laden m.	shop
Laib m.	loaf
Lamm n.	lamb
landen	to land
Landkarte f.	map
Landstraße f.	highway
lang	long
langsam	slow
langweilig	boring
Laptop m.	laptop
lassen	to let
Lastwagen m.	truck
laufen	to run
laufende Nase	runny nose
Lebenslauf m.	resume
Lebensmittelgeschäft n.	grocery store
Lehrer m., *Lehrerin* f.	teacher
leicht	light, easy, mild
Leid n.	sorrow

leiden	to suffer
Leid tun (sich)	to be sorry
Lenkrad n.	steering wheel
lerneifrig	studious
lesen	to read
leugnen	to deny
lieben	to love
Likör m.	liqueur
Limonade f.	lemonade
Limone f.	lime
links	left
Lippe f.	lip
Liter n.	liter
Loch n.	cavity, hole
locken (sich)	to curl
Löffel m.	spoon
Loge f.	box (theater)
Lohn m.	salary, wage
Lohnerhöhung f.	raise, salary increase
lose	loose, slack
löschen	to delete (computer file)
Luftpost f.	airmail
Luxuswagen m.	luxury car
lyrisch	lyrical
machen	to make, do
Mädchen n.	girl
Magen m.	stomach
Magenschmerzen pl.	stomachache
Mahlzeit f.	meal
Mai m.	May
Mais m.	corn
man	one, someone
Manager m., *Managerin* f.	manager
Mandel f.	almond
Mann m.	man, husband
Männerkleidung f.	men's clothing
Manschettenknopf m.	cufflink
Mantel m.	coat, overcoat
Mappe f.	briefcase, folder
Markt m.	market
Marmelade f.	jam, marmelade
März m.	March
Maus f.	mouse
Mechaniker m., *Mechanikerin* f.	mechanic
mechanisch	mechanical

Medikament n.	medication
mehr	more
mein	my
Messer n.	knife
Metzgerei f.	butcher shop
Mexikaner m., *Mexikanerin* f.	Mexican (person)
mexikanisch	Mexican
Milch f.	milk
Milchladen m.	dairy store
Milchzahn m.	baby tooth
mild	mild
Milliarde f.	billion
Milliliter n.	milliliter
Million f.	million
Mindestlohn m.	minimum wage
Mineralwasser n.	mineral water
Minirock m.	miniskirt
Minute f.	minute
mit	with
Mittag m.	noon
Mittagessen n.	lunch
mittelgroß	medium (size)
Mitternacht f.	midnight
Mittwoch m.	Wednesday
Mobiltelefon n.	mobile telephone
mögen	to like, want to
Möhre f.	carrot
Monitor m.	monitor
Montag m.	Monday
Moped n.	moped
morgen	tomorrow
Morgen m.	morning
müde	tired
Münze f.	coin
müssen	must, to have to
Mund m.	mouth
Muscheln pl.	mussels
Museum n.	museum
Musik f.	music
Mutter f.	mother
nach	after, to
nach Hause	home(ward)
Nachgebühr f.	postage due, surcharge
Nachname m.	last name
Nachricht f.	message

nachschicken	to forward
nächste	next
Nacht f.	night
Nachtisch m.	dessert
nah	near
naiv	naive
Name m.	name
Nase f.	nose
national	national
Natur f.	nature
neben	next to
neblig	foggy
Neffe m.	nephew
negativ	negative
nein	no
nervös	nervous
neu	new
neun	nine
neunzehn	nineteen
neunzig	ninety
nicht	not
Nichte f.	niece
nichts	nothing
nie	never
Niederländer m., *Niederländerin* f.	Dutchman, Dutchwoman
niedrig	low
niemals	never
niemand	no one
niesen	to sneeze
noch	still
Norden m.	north
Normalbenzin n.	regular gas
Note f.	grade; note
Notfall m.	emergency
November m.	November
Nudeln pl.	noodles
Nummer f.	number
nur	only
ob	whether, if
oben	above
Obst n.	fruit
Obstkuchen m.	pie
oder	or
offen	open
offensiv	offensive

öffentlich	public ·
öffnen	to open
ohne	without
Ohnmacht f.	faint
Ohr n.	ear
Ohrenschmerzen pl.	earache
Ohrring m.	earring
Oktober m.	October
Onkel m.	uncle
Oper f.	opera
Optimist m.	optimist
Orange f., *orange*	orange
Orchester n.	orchestra
Orgel f.	organ (musical instrument)
örtlich	local
Ortsgespräch n.	local call
Osten m.	east
Österreicher m., *Österreicherin*, f.	Austrian
Paket n.	package
Pampelmuse f.	grapefruit
Panne f.	flat tire, breakdown
Papier n.	paper
Parfüm n.	perfume
Park m.	park
parken	to park
Parkplatz m.	parking lot
Party f.	party
Pass m.	passport
Passagier m.	passenger
Passkontrolle f.	passport control (immigration)
patriotisch	patriotic
Pendelbus m.	shuttle bus
Penizillin n.	penicillin
Pension f.	boarding house
perfekt	perfect
Person f.	person
Pessimist m.	pessimist
Petersilie f.	parsley
Pfeffer m.	pepper
Pfirsich m.	peach
Pflaume f.	plum
Pförtner m., *Pförtnerin* f.	doorman
Pfund n.	pound (weight/money)
Pille f.	pill
Pilot m., *Pilotin* f.	pilot

Pilz m.	mushroom
Platz m.	seat
Plätzchen n.	cookie
Pole m., *Polin* f.	Pole, Polish person
politisch	political
Polizei m.	police
Polizeistation f.	police station
Polizist m., *Polizistin* f.	police officer
Pommes frites pl.	french fries
populär	popular
Porto n.	postage
positiv	positive
Post f.	mail, post office
Postamt n.	post office
Postanweisung f.	money order
Posteingang m.	inbox, incoming mail
Postkarte f.	postcard
postlagernd	general delivery
Postleitzahl f.	zip code
Präsident m., *Präsidentin* f.	president
pro	per
Problem n.	problem
Professor m., *Professorin* f.	professor
promovieren	to earn a doctorate
prost	cheers
Pudding m.	pudding
Pullover m.	sweater
putzen	to clean, polish
Quark m.	curd cheese, quark
Quittung f.	receipt
radfahren	to cycle, ride a bike
Radiergummi m.	eraser
rasieren (sich)	to shave (oneself)
Rathaus n.	city hall
Ratte f.	rat
rauchen	to smoke
reagieren	to react
Rechner m.	calculator
Rechnung f.	bill
rechts	right
Rechtsanwalt m., *Rechtsanwältin* f.	lawyer
Regen m.	rain
Regenmantel m.	raincoat
Regenschirm m.	umbrella
regnen	to rain

regnerisch	rainy
reinigen	to clean
Reis m.	rice
Reisescheck m.	traveler's check
relativ	relative
Reparatur f.	repair
reparieren	to repair
Republik f.	republic
Reservierung f.	reservation
Restaurant n.	restaurant
Rezept n.	prescription
Rezeption f.	reception (front desk)
R-Gespräch n.	collect call
rhythmisch	rhythmic
Rinderbraten m.	roast beef
Ring m.	ring
Rock m.	skirt
Roggenbrot n.	rye bread
Rollschuh laufen	to roller-skate
romantisch	romantic
rosa	pink
Rose f.	rose
Ross n.	horse, steed
rot	red
Rucksack m.	backpack
rudern	to row
Rücken m.	back
ruhig	calm, quiet
Russe m., *Russin* f.	Russian
Saft m.	juice
sagen	to say
Sahne f.	cream
Sakko m.	sports coat
Salat m.	salad
Salz n.	salt
Samstag m.	Saturday
Sandalen pl.	sandals
satt	full, satiated
Sauerrahm m.	sour cream
S-Bahn f.	city and suburban railway
Scanner m.	scanner
Schach n.	chess
Schachtel f.	box
Schaf n.	sheep
schaffen	to create, get done

Schal m.	scarf, muffler
Schale f.	bowl
Schalter m.	counter, window
Schauspieler m., *Schauspielerin* f.	actor
Scheck m.	check
Scheckbuch n.	checkbook
Scheibenwischer m.	windshield wiper
Scheinwerfer m.	headlight
scherzhaft	joking, playful
Schinken m.	ham
Schlafanzug m.	pajamas
schlafen	to sleep
Schlaflosigkeit f.	insomnia
Schlägerei f.	fistfight, brawl
schlampig	sloppy
schlecht	bad
Schlips m.	tie
Schlüpfer m.	panties
Schmuck m.	jewelry
schneiden	to cut
schneien	to snow
schnell	fast
Schnellimbiss m.	snack bar
Schokolade f.	chocolate
schon	already
schön	pretty, nice
schreiben	to write
Schreibmaschine f.	typewriter
Schreibtisch m.	desk
Schriftsteller m., *Schriftstellerin* f.	writer
schüchtern	shy
Schuhe pl.	shoes
Schuhgröße f.	shoe size
Schularbeit f.	homework
Schule f.	school
Schüler m., *Schülerin* f.	pupil
Schulter f.	shoulder
Schultertuch n.	shawl
Schuss m.	shot
schwach	weak
schwanger	pregnant
schwarz	black
Schwarzbrot n.	black bread
Schwede m., *Schwedin* f.	Swede
Schwein n.	pig

Schweinefleisch n.	pork
Schweizer m., *Schweizerin* f.	Swiss
schwer	hard, heavy
Schwester f.	sister
Schwimmbad n.	swimming pool
schwimmen	to swim
schwindlig	dizzy
sechs	six
sechzehn	sixteen
sechzig	sixty
See f.	sea
See m.	lake
seekrank	seasick
Seekrankheit f.	seasickness
segeln	to sail
sehen	to see
sehr	very
Seife f.	soap
sein	his
sein	to be
Sekretär m., *Sekretärin* f.	secretary
Sekt m.	sparkling wine, champagne
Selterswasser n.	sparkling water
senden	to send
Senf m.	mustard
September m.	September
Service m.	service
Serviette f.	napkin
setzen (sich)	to seat (oneself)
Sicherheitskontrolle f.	security check
Sie	you (formal)
sie pl.	they
sie sing.	she, her, it
sieben	seven
siebzehn	seventeen
siebzig	seventy
siezen	to say *Sie* to (address formally)
Sinfonie f.	symphony
singen	to sing
Sinusitis f.	sinusitis
Skijacke f.	ski jacket
Ski laufen	to ski
Smoking m.	tuxedo
Snack m.	snack
Socke f.	sock

Sodbrennen n.	heartburn
Sofa n.	sofa
sofort	immediately
Software f.	software
Sohn m.	son
solid	solid
sollen	should
Sommer m.	summer
Sommersprossen pl.	freckles
Sonnabend m.	Saturday
Sonnenbrand m.	sunburn
Sonnenbrille f.	sunglasses
sonnengebräunt	tan
sonnig	sunny
Sonntag m.	Sunday
soviel	as much
sozialistisch	socialistic
Spanier m., *Spanierin* f.	Spaniard
sparen	to save
Spargel m.	asparagus
Sparkasse f.	savings bank
Sparkonto n.	savings account
Spaß m.	fun
spät	late
spazieren	to stroll
Speisekarte f.	menu
Spende f.	donation
spielen	to play
Spielfilm m.	feature film
Spinat m.	spinach
Spinne f.	spider
sportlich	athletic, sporty
sprechen	to speak
Spritze f.	injection, shot
Sprudelwasser n.	carbonated water
spülen	to rinse
Stadt f.	city
Stangensellerie m.	celery
stark	strong
Stärke f.	starch; strength
starten	to take off (aircraft)
Statistik f.	statistic
Steak n.	steak
Stein m.	rock, stone
Stiefel m.	boot

Stil m.	style
stimmen	to be correct
stören	to disturb
Straße f.	street
Straßenraub m.	mugging
strikt	strict
Strom m.	torrent; current (electricity)
Strumpf m.	stocking
Strumpfhose f.	pantyhose, tights
Student m., *Studentin* f.	student
Stück n.	piece
stürmisch	stormy
Stuhl m.	chair
Stunde f.	hour
suchen	to look for, seek
Süden m.	south
Süßigkeiten pl.	candy
Süßwarengeschäft n.	candy store
Summe f.	sum
Supermarkt m.	supermarket
Suppe f.	soup
sympathisch	likeable
synchronisiert	dubbed
System n.	system
Tabakwarenhändler m.	tobacco shop
Tablett n.	tray
Tablette f.	tablet, pill
Tag m.	day
tanken	to fill up (gas tank)
Tankstelle f.	gas station
Tante f.	aunt
tanzen	to dance
tapfer	brave
Taschentuch n.	handkerchief
Tasse f.	cup
Tastatur f.	keyboard
tausend	thousand
Taxi n.	taxi
Taxistand m.	taxi stand
Tee m.	tea
Telefon n.	telephone
Telefonbuch n.	telephone book
telefonieren	to telephone, call up
Teller m.	plate
Tennis n.	tennis

teuer	expensive
Textmarker m.	highlighter
Theater n.	theater
Tier n.	animal
Tisch m.	table
Tischler m., *Tischlerin* f.	carpenter
Tochter f.	daughter
Toilette f.	toilet, restroom
Tomate f.	tomato
Topf m.	pot, jar
Torte f.	torte, tart, flan
total	total
tragbar	portable
tragen	to carry, wear
trampen	to hitchhike
Transport m.	transportation
traurig	sad
Treffen n.	meeting
trinken	to drink
Trinkgeld n.	tip, gratuity
Tritt m.	kick
trocknen	to dry
Trockner m.	dryer
Trompete f.	trumpet
Truthahn m.	turkey
tschüs	so long, bye
T-Shirt n.	T-shirt
Tür f.	door
tun	to do
Turnschuhe pl.	gym shoes, sneakers
U-Bahn f.	subway
überholen	to pass
überqueren	to cross
Überschwemmung f.	flood
Uhr f.	clock
um	around
Umweg m.	detour
umziehen (sich)	to change clothes
und	and
Unfall m.	accident
ungeduldig	impatient
Unglück n.	crash, accident
Universität f.	university
unser	our
Unsinn m.	nonsense

unten	below
unter	under
unterbrochen	interrupted
Unterhemd n.	undershirt
Unterkunft f.	accomodation
Unterrock m.	slip
unterschreiben	to sign
Untertasse f.	saucer
Untertitel m.	subtitle
Unterwäsche f.	underwear
unterwegs	on the way
Ursache f.	cause
Vanille f.	vanilla
Vase f.	vase
Vater m.	father
Vegetarier m.	vegetarian
verbinden	to connect
verdienen	to earn
vergesslich	forgetful
Vergewaltigung f.	rape
verkaufen	to sell
Verkehrsampel f.	traffic light
Verkehrsstau m.	traffic jam
verlangsamen	to slow down
verlegen	embarrassed
verletzen	to injure
verleugnen	to deny
verlieren	to lose
verloben (sich)	to get engaged
Verlobte m./f.	fiancé, financée
Verlobungsring m.	engagement ring
versichern	to insure
Versicherung f.	insurance
verstehen	to understand
Verstopfung f.	constipation
Vertrag m.	contract
verwirrt	confused
verwunden	to wound
verzeihen	to forgive
Verzeihung f.	forgiveness; excuse me
verzollen	to declare
viel	much
viele	many
vier	four
Vierradantrieb m.	four-wheel drive

Viertel n.	quarter
vierzehn	fourteen
vierzig	forty
Visum n.	visa
Vogel m.	bird
Vöglein n.	little bird
Volleyball m.	volleyball
Vollkornbrot n.	whole-wheat bread
von	from, of
vor	before, in front of
vorbeifahren	to drive past
vorder	front
Vorführung f.	presentation, performance
Vorname m.	first name
Vorsicht f.	caution
Vorspeise f.	appetizer, starter
vorstellen	to introduce
Vorstellung f.	presentation, performance; introduction
Vorstellungsgespräch n.	interview
vorübergehend	temporary
Vorwahl f.	area code
Wagen m.	car
wählen	to dial
Wählton m.	dial tone
während	during
wandern	to hike
Wandtafel f.	blackboard
Wange f.	cheek
wann	when
warm	warm
warum	why
was	what
Wäschedienst m.	laundry service
waschen (sich)	to wash (oneself)
Wäscherei f.	laundry, laundromat
Waschmaschine f.	washing machine
Waschmittel n.	detergent
Wasser n.	water
Wasserski laufen	to water ski
Website f.	website
Wechselkurs m.	exchange rate
wechseln	to exchange
Wechselstube f.	currency exchange
Weckanruf m.	wake-up call
wegen	because of

weh tun	to hurt
Wehen bekommen	to go into labor
Weichspülmittel n.	fabric softener
Wein m.	wine
Weinglas n.	wineglass
Weintraube f.	grape
Weisheitszahn m.	wisdom tooth
weiß	white
weit	far
welcher, welche, welches	which
wenig	little (amount)
weniger	less, fewer
wenn	whenever, if
wer	who
werden	to become, get; shall, will
Westen m.	west
Wetter n.	weather
wie	how
wieder	again
wiederholen	to repeat
wiegen	to weigh
windig	windy
Windschutzscheibe f.	windshield
Winter m.	winter
wir	we
Wirkung f.	effect
wissen	to know
WLAN n.	Wi-Fi, WLAN
wo	where
Woche f.	week
wohin	where (to)
wohl	well
Wohnung f.	apartment
wollen	to want
Wörterbuch n.	dictionary
Wurst f.	sausage
Wurzelbehandlung f.	root canal
zahlen	to pay
zählen	to count
Zahn m.	tooth
Zahnarzt m., *Zahnärztin* f.	dentist
Zahnbürste f.	toothbrush
Zahnfleisch n.	gum
Zahnfüllung f.	filling (dental)
Zahnkrone f.	crown (dental)

Zahnprothese f.	dentures
Zahnreinigung f.	teeth cleaning
Zahnseide f.	dental floss
Zahnweh n.	toothache
Zeh m.	toe
zehn	ten
zeigen	to show
Zeit f.	time
Zeitumstellung f.	jet lag; time change
Zeitung f.	newspaper
Zeitungskiosk m.	newspaper stand
Zelt n.	tent
Zimmer frei	bed and breakfast; vacancies
Zimmer n.	room
Zinssatz m.	interest rate
Zitrone f.	lemon
Zoll m.	customs duty
Zoo m.	zoo
zu	to
zu Hause	at home
Zucker m.	sugar
Zug m.	train
Zugang m.	admittance
Zugfahrplan m.	train schedule
zurückbleiben	to stand back
zurückbringen	to bring back
zurückhaltend	reserved, guarded
Zusammenstoß m.	crash
zuversichtlich	confident
zwanzig	twenty
zwei	two
Zwiebel f.	onion
Zwischenlandung f.	stopover
zwölf	twelve

Appendix B

English–German Dictionary

The gender and number of the nouns listed here are indicated by m. for masculine, f. for feminine, n. for neuter, sing. for singular, and pl. for plural. Both German and English verbs are provided as infinitives.

a, an	*ein, eine*
above	*oben*
abscess	*Abszess* m.
abstract	*abstrakt*
to accelerate	*beschleunigen*
accent	*Akzent* m.
accident	*Unfall* m.
accommodation	*Unterkunft* f.
acquaintance	*Bekannte* m./f.
active	*aktiv*
actor	*Schauspieler* m., *Schauspielerin* f.
address	*Adresse* f., *Anschrift* f.
admittance	*Zugang* m.
African	*Afrikaner* m., *Afrikanerin* f.
after	*nach*
again	*wieder*
against	*gegen*
against it	*dagegen*
air conditioning	*Klimaanlage* f.
airline	*Fluggesellschaft* f.
airline passenger	*Fluggast* m.
airline ticket	*Flugticket* n.
airmail	*Luftpost* f.
airplane	*Flugzeug* n.
airport	*Flughafen* m.
all, everyone	*alle*
allergic	*allergisch*
allergy	*Allergie* f.
almond	*Mandel* f.
alone	*allein*
already	*schon*
also, too	*auch*
always	*immer*
ambulance	*Krankenwagen* m.
America	*Amerika* n.
American	*Amerikaner* m., *Amerikanerin* f.
and	*und*
anesthesia, anesthetic	*Betäubung* f., *Betäubungsmittel* n.
angry	*böse*
animal	*Tier* n.
ankle	*Fußgelenk* n.
annoyed, annoying	*ärgerlich*
to answer (the phone); withdraw (from an account)	*abheben*
answering machine	*Anrufbeantworter* m.

antibiotic	*Antibiotikum* n.
apartment	*Wohnung* f.
ape, monkey	*Affe* m.
apparatus, appliance	*Apparat* m.
appetite	*Appetit* m.
appetizer, starter	*Vorspeise* f.
apple	*Apfel* m.
to apply for	*bewerben (sich)*
apricot	*Aprikose* f.
April	*April* m.
area code	*Vorwahl* f.
arm	*Arm* m.
around	*um*
arrival	*Ankunft* f.
arthritis	*Arthritis* f.
artichoke	*Artischocke* f.
artist	*Artist* m., *Artistin* f.; *Künstler* m., *Künstlerin* f.
as if	*als ob*
as much	*soviel*
ashamed	*beschämt*
to ask	*fragen*
asparagus	*Spargel* m.
aspirin	*Aspirin* n.
asthmatic	*asthmatisch*
asthmatic (person)	*Asthmatiker* m.
at all	*gar*
at home	*zu Hause*
athletic	*athletisch*
athletic, sporty	*sportlich*
ATM	*Geldautomat* m.
attack	*Angriff* m.
attractive	*attraktiv*
August	*August* m.
aunt	*Tante* f.
Austrian	*Österreicher* m., *Österreicherin* f.
auto	*Auto* n.
automatic transmission	*Automatikgetriebe* n.
automobile	*Automobil* n.
autumn	*Herbst* m.
baby	*Baby* n.
baby tooth	*Milchzahn* m.
back	*Rücken* m.
backpack	*Rucksack* m.
bad	*schlecht*

baggage claim	*Gepäckausgabe* f.
baggage, luggage	*Gepäck* n.
baker	*Bäcker* m., *Bäckerin* f.
bakery	*Bäckerei* f.
balcony	*Balkon* m.
ballet	*Ballett* n.
banana	*Banane* f.
bank	*Bank* f.
bank balance	*Kontostand* m.
bank statement	*Kontoauszug* m.
barber, hair stylist	*Friseur* m.
barrette	*Haarspange* f.
baseball	*Baseball* m.
basement, cellar	*Keller* m.
basketball	*Basketball* m., *Korbball* m.
bathing suit, swimsuit	*Badeanzug* m.
bathtub	*Badewanne* f.
Brazilian	*Brasilianer* m., *Brasilianerin* f.
to be	*sein*
to be afraid	*Angst haben*
to be called	*heißen*
to be correct	*stimmen*
to be glad, happy	*freuen (sich)*
to be sorry	*Leid tun (sich)*
bean	*Bohne* f.
bear	*Bär* m.
beautiful, handsome	*hübsch*
because	*denn*
because of	*wegen*
to become acquainted	*kennen lernen*
to become, get; shall, will	*werden*
bed	*Bett* n.
bed and breakfast; vacancies	*Zimmer frei*
beer	*Bier* n.
before, in front of	*vor*
to behave	*benehmen (sich)*
behind, in back of	*hinter*
below	*unten*
belt	*Gürtel* m.
bicycle	*Fahrrad* n.
big, large, tall	*groß*
bikini	*Bikini* m.
bill	*Rechnung* f.
bill, paper money	*Geldschein* m.
billion	*Milliarde* f.

bird	*Vogel* m.
black	*schwarz*
black bread	*Schwarzbrot* n.
blackberry	*Brombeere* f.
blackboard	*Wandtafel* f.
bleach	*Bleichmittel* n.
to bleed	*bluten*
blind	*blind*
blood pressure	*Blutdruck* m.
blouse	*Bluse* f.
to blow-dry	*fönen*
blue	*blau*
blueberry	*Blaubeere* f., *Heidelbeere* f.
boarding house	*Pension* f.
boarding pass	*Bordkarte* f., *Einsteigekarte* f.
boat	*Boot* n.
book	*Buch* n.
book of stamps	*Briefmarkenheft* n.
boot	*Stiefel* m.
boring	*langweilig*
boss	*Chef* m., *Chefin* f.
bottle	*Flasche* f.
bow tie; fly	*Fliege* f.
bowl	*Schale* f.
box	*Schachtel* f.
box (theater)	*Loge* f.
boxer shorts	*Boxershorts* pl.
boy	*Junge* m.
bra	*BH* m.
bracelet	*Armband* n.
brake	*Bremse* f.
brake light	*Bremslicht* n.
brassiere	*Büstenhalter* m.
brave	*tapfer*
bread	*Brot* n.
to break	*brechen*
breakfast	*Frühstück* n.
bride	*Braut* f.
briefcase	*Aktentasche* f.
briefcase, folder	*Mappe* f.
to bring back	*zurückbringen*
broach	*Brosche* f.
broken	*kaputt*
brother	*Bruder* m.
brown	*braun*

to brush	*bürsten*
burglary, break-in	*Diebstahl* m., *Einbruch* m.
bus	*Bus* m.
bus station	*Busbahnhof* m.
bus stop	*Bushaltestelle* f.
business card	*Geschäftskarte* f.
busy, engaged (phone)	*besetzt*
but	*aber*
but, still	*doch*
butcher	*Fleischer* m., *Fleischerin* f.
butcher shop	*Fleischerei* f., *Metzgerei* f.
butter	*Butter* f.
buttermilk	*Buttermilch* f.
to buy	*kaufen*
by, at	*bei*
cake	*Kuchen* m.
calculator	*Rechner* m.
calf	*Kalb* n.
to call (phone)	*anrufen, telefonieren*
can	*Büchse* f., *Dose* f.
can, to be able to	*können*
Canadian	*Kanadier* m., *Kanadierin* f.
candy	*Süßigkeiten* pl.
candy store	*Süßwarengeschäft* n.
canine tooth	*Eckzahn* m.
capitalist	*Kapitalist* m.
car	*Wagen* m.
carbonated water	*Sprudelwasser* n.
cards (playing)	*Karten* pl.
carpenter	*Tischler* m., *Tischlerin* f.
carrot	*Karotte* f., *Möhre* f.
to carry, wear	*tragen*
carry-on luggage	*Handgepäck* n.
cash	*Bargeld* n.
to cash (in)	*einlösen*
to catch a cold	*erkälten (sich)*
cauliflower	*Blumenkohl* m.
cause	*Ursache* f.
caution	*Vorsicht* f.
cavity, hole	*Loch* n.
CD-ROM drive	*CD-ROM-Laufwerk* n.
celebration	*Fest* n.
celery	*Stangensellerie* m.
cell phone	*Handy* n.
CEO	*Generaldirektor* m.

certified	*bestätigt*
chain	*Kette* f.
chair	*Stuhl* m.
chalk	*Kreide* f.
chance	*Chance* f.
change (money)	*Kleingeld* n.
change, alteration	*Änderung* f.
to change clothes	*umziehen (sich)*
cheap	*billig*
check	*Scheck* m.
to check in (luggage)	*abfertigen, aufgeben*
checkbook	*Scheckbuch* n.
check-in counter	*Abfertigungsschalter* m.
checking account	*Girokonto* n.
cheek	*Backe* f., *Wange* f.
cheers	*prost*
cheese	*Käse* m.
cherry	*Kirsche* f.
chess	*Schach* n.
chest	*Brust* f.
chicken	*Hähnchen* n., *Huhn* n.
child	*Kind* n.
chocolate	*Schokolade* f.
church	*Kirche* f.
city	*Stadt* f.
city and suburban railway	*S-Bahn* f.
city hall	*Rathaus* n.
civil servant, official	*Beamte* m., *Beamtin* f.
class	*Klasse* f.
classroom	*Klassenzimmer* n.
to clean	*reinigen*
to clean, polish	*putzen*
to click on	*anklicken*
clock	*Uhr* f.
clothing store	*Bekleidungsgeschäft* n.
coat, overcoat	*Mantel* m.
cocktail	*Cocktail* m.
cocoa	*Kakao* m.
coffee	*Kaffee* m.
coin	*Münze* f.
cold (illness)	*Erkältung* f.
cold (temperature)	*kalt*
collect call	*R-Gespräch* n.
color	*Farbe* f.
to color, dye	*färben*

to come	*kommen*
communist	*kommunistisch*
compact car	*Kompaktwagen* m.
company	*Firma* f.
computer	*Computer* m.
conceited	*eingebildet*
concert	*Konzert* n.
conference	*Konferenz* f.
confident	*zuversichtlich*
confused	*verwirrt*
to connect	*verbinden*
constipation	*Verstopfung* f.
contract	*Vertrag* m.
convertible	*Kabrio* n.
cook	*Koch* m., *Köchin* f.
to cook	*kochen*
cookie	*Plätzchen* n.
cool	*kühl*
copy machine	*Kopiergerät* n.
corn	*Mais* m.
correct	*korrekt*
corridor	*Korridor* m.
to cost	*kosten*
cough drop	*Hustenbonbon* n.
cough syrup	*Hustensaft* m.
to count	*zählen*
counter, window	*Schalter* m.
course (school)	*Kursus* m.
cousin	*Cousin* m., *Cousine* f.
cow	*Kuh* f.
cowardly	*feige*
cozy, comfortable	*gemütlich*
crash, accident	*Unglück* n., *Zusammenstoß* m.
cream	*Sahne* f.
cream cheese	*Frischkäse* m.
to create, get done	*schaffen*
credit card	*Kreditkarte* f.
critical	*kritisch*
to cross	*überqueren*
crown (dental)	*Zahnkrone* f.
cucumber	*Gurke* f.
cufflink	*Manschettenknopf* m.
cummerbund	*Kummerbund* m.
cup	*Tasse* f.
to curl	*locken (sich)*

currency exchange	*Geldwechsel* m., *Wechselstube* f.
customs duty	*Zoll* m.
to cut	*schneiden*
cybercafé	*Cybercafé* n.
to cycle, ride a bike	*radfahren*
dairy store	*Milchladen* m.
to dance	*tanzen*
dark blue	*dunkelblau*
daughter	*Tochter* f.
day	*Tag* m.
December	*Dezember* m.
to declare	*verzollen*
to declare; to explain	*erklären*
to delete (computer file)	*löschen*
democratic	*demokratisch*
dental floss	*Zahnseide* f.
dentist	*Zahnarzt* m., *Zahnärztin* f.
dentures	*Zahnprothese* f.
to deny	*leugnen, verleugnen*
department (school)	*Fakultät* f.
department store	*Kaufhaus* n.
departure	*Abreise* f.
departure (plane)	*Abflug* m.
to deposit (money)	*einzahlen*
desk	*Schreibtisch* m.
dessert	*Nachtisch* m.
detergent	*Waschmittel* n.
detour	*Umweg* m.
diabetic (person)	*Diabetiker* m., *Diabetikerin* f.
diabetic	*diabetisch*
to dial	*wählen*
dial tone	*Wählton* m.
diarrhea	*Durchfall* m.
dictionary	*Wörterbuch* n.
diet	*Diät* f.
diligent, hard-working	*fleißig*
dimple	*Grübchen* n.
dining room	*Esszimmer* n.
dinner, supper	*Abendbrot* n., *Abendessen* n.
diplomat	*Diplomat* m., *Diplomatin* f.
disappointed	*enttäuscht*
to disturb	*stören*
dizzy	*schwindlig*
to do	*tun*
doctor, physician	*Arzt* m., *Ärztin* f.

doctorate	*Doktorgrad* m.
donation	*Spende* f.
don't mention it	*keine Ursache*
door	*Tür* f.
doorman	*Pförtner* m., *Pförtnerin* f.
double bed	*Doppelbett* n.
doughnut	*Berliner* m.
to download	*downloaden, herunterladen*
dress	*Kleid* n.
to dress (oneself)	*anziehen (sich)*
dress size, clothing size	*Kleidergröße* f.
drink, beverage	*Getränk* n.
to drink	*trinken*
to drive, go (by)	*fahren (mit)*
to drive past	*vorbeifahren*
drive, trip	*Fahrt* f.
driver	*Fahrer* m., *Fahrerin* f.
to drown	*ertrinken*
drugstore, pharmacy	*Drogerie* f., *Apotheke* f.
to dry	*trocknen*
dry cleaner	*chemische Reinigung* f.
dryer	*Trockner* m.
dubbed (in)	*synchronisiert*
during	*während*
Dutchman, Dutchwoman	*Niederländer* m., *Niederländerin* f.
each	*jeder, jede, jedes*
ear	*Ohr* n.
earache	*Ohrenschmerzen* pl.
early	*früh*
to earn	*verdienen*
to earn a doctorate	*promovieren*
earring	*Ohrring* m.
east	*Osten* m.
to eat	*essen*
economy car	*Economywagen* m.
effect	*Wirkung* f.
effective	*effektiv*
egg	*Ei* n.
Egyptian	*Ägypter* m., *Ägypterin* f.
eight	*acht*
eighteeen	*achtzehn*
eighty	*achtzig*
elbow	*Ellbogen* m.
electrician	*Elektriker* m., *Elektrikerin* f.
elephant	*Elefant* m.

elevator	*Fahrstuhl* m.
eleven	*elf*
e-mail	*E-Mail* f.
e-mail address	*E-Mail-Adresse* f.
embarrassed	*verlegen*
emergency	*Notfall* m.
to employ	*einstellen*
employee	*Angestellte* m./f.
enemy	*Feind* m.
engagement ring	*Verlobungsring* m.
engineer	*Ingenieur* m., *Ingenieurin* f.
England	*England*
English	*englisch*
Englishman, Englishwoman	*Engländer* m., *Engländerin* f.
enough	*genug*
envelope	*Briefumschlag* m.
equal, same	*gleich*
eraser	*Radiergummi* m.
European	*Europäer* m., *Europäerin* f.
evening	*Abend* m.
everything	*alles*
exam	*Examen* n.
to exchange	*wechseln*
exchange rate	*Wechselkurs* m.
excited	*aufgeregt*
excuse	*Entschuldigung* f.
exhausted	*erschöpft*
expensive	*teuer*
explosion	*Explosion* f.
express delivery	*Eilzustellung* f.
express letter	*Eilbrief* m.
to extract	*extrahieren*
eye	*Auge* n.
eye tooth	*Augenzahn* m.
eyeglasses	*Brille* f.
face	*Gesicht* n.
faint	*Ohnmacht* f.
fair	*fair*
to fall	*fallen*
false	*falsch*
family	*Familie* f.
far	*weit*
farmhand	*Knecht* m.
fast	*schnell*
fat	*Fett* n.

fat, thick	*dick*
father	*Vater* m.
favor	*Gefallen* m.
fax machine	*Faxgerät* n.
feature film	*Spielfilm* m.
February	*Februar* m.
fee, toll	*Gebühr* f.
felt	*Filz* m.
fever	*Fieber* n.
fiancé, fiancée	*Verlobte* m./f.
field	*Feld* n.
fifteen	*fünfzehn*
fifty	*fünfzig*
file	*Datei* f.
filing cabinet	*Aktenschrank* m.
to fill up (gas tank)	*tanken*
filling	*Zahnfüllung* f.
film, movie	*Film* m.
to find	*finden*
finger	*Finger* m.
fingernail	*Fingernagel* m.
fire	*Feuer* n.
to fire, dismiss	*entlassen*
firefighter	*Feuerwehrfrau* f., *Feuerwehrmann* m.
first floor (U.S.), ground floor (UK)	*Erdgeschoss* n.
first name	*Vorname* m.
fish	*Fisch* m.
to fish	*fischen, angeln*
fish market	*Fischgeschäft* n.
fistfight, brawl	*Schlägerei* f.
five	*fünf*
fixed menu	*Gedeck* n.
to flash (lightning)	*blitzen*
flat tire, breakdown	*Panne* f.
flight	*Flug* m.
flood	*Überschwemmung* f.
floppy disk	*Floppy Disk* f.
flower	*Blume* f.
flu	*Grippe* f.
flute	*Flöte* f.
to fly	*fliegen*
foggy	*neblig*
foot	*Fuß* m.
for	*für*
forgetful	*vergesslich*

to forgive	*verzeihen*
forgiveness; excuse me	*Verzeihung* f.
fork	*Gabel* f.
forty	*vierzig*
to forward	*nachschicken*
four	*vier*
fourteen	*vierzehn*
four-wheel drive	*Vierradantrieb* m.
freckles	*Sommersprossen* pl.
french fries	*Pommes frites* pl.
Frenchman, Frenchwoman	*Franzose* m., *Französin* f.
frequent	*häufig*
fresh	*frisch*
Friday	*Freitag* m.
friend, boyfriend/girlfriend	*Freund* m., *Freundin* f.
friendly	*freundschaftlich*
frog	*Frosch* m.
from, of	*von*
front	*vorder*
frostbite	*Erfrierungen* pl.
fruit	*Obst* n.
full, satiated	*satt*
fun	*Spaß* m.
funny	*komisch*
gain, yield (financial)	*Ertrag* m.
garage	*Garage* f.
garden	*Garten* m.
to garden	*gärtnern*
gardening	*Gartenarbeit* f.
gardner	*Gärtner* m., *Gartnerin* f.
gas	*Gas* n.
gas pedal	*Gaspedal* n.
gas station	*Tankstelle* f.
gasoline	*Benzin* n.
gate (airport)	*Flugsteig* m.
general delivery	*postlagernd*
generous	*großzügig*
German	*deutsch*
German (person)	*Deutsche* m./f.
Germany	*Deutschland*
to get engaged	*verloben (sich)*
to get, fetch	*holen*
girl	*Mädchen* n.
to give	*geben*
to give up; check in (luggage)	*aufgeben*

gladly	*gern*
glass, jar	*Glas* n.
gloves	*Handschuhe* pl.
to go (on foot)	*gehen*
to go into labor	*Wehen bekommen*
golf	*Golf* n.
good, well	*gut*
goodbye	*auf Wiedersehen*
goodbye (on the phone)	*auf Wiederhören*
grade; note	*Note* f.
grade (year in school)	*Klasse* f.
gram	*Gramm* n.
grandchild	*Enkel* m., *Enkelin* f.
grandfather	*Großvater* m.
grandmother	*Großmutter* f.
grape	*Weintraube* f.
grapefruit	*Pampelmuse* f.
grave	*Grab* n.
gray	*grau*
green	*grün*
to greet	*grüßen*
grocery store	*Lebensmittelgeschäft* n.
groom	*Bräutigam* m.
guitar	*Gitarre* f.
gum	*Zahnfleisch* n.
gym shoes, sneakers	*Turnschuhe* pl.
to habilitate, qualify as a professor	*habilitieren*
hair	*Haar* n.
hairdo	*Frisur* f.
half	*halb*
hallway	*Flur, Korridor* m.
ham	*Schinken* m.
hand	*Hand* f.
to hand in	*abgeben*
handbag, purse	*Handtasche* f.
handkerchief	*Taschentuch* n.
to hang up (phone)	*aufhängen*
to happen	*geschehen*
happy	*froh*
hard	*hart*
hard drive	*Festplattenlaufwerk* n.
hardware (computer)	*Hardware* f.
hat	*Hut* m.
to have	*haben*
hay fever	*Heuschnupfen* m.

he, it (m.)	*er*
head	*Kopf* m.
headache	*Kopfschmerzen* pl.
headlight	*Scheinwerfer* m.
health; bless you (after a sneeze)	*Gesundheit* f.
healthy	*gesund*
to hear	*hören*
heart	*Herz* n.
heartburn	*Sodbrennen* n.
heat	*Hitze* f.
to heat	*heizen*
heavy, hard	*schwer*
help, aid	*Hilfe* f.
to help	*helfen*
hemorrhoids	*Hämorrhoiden* pl.
her	*ihr*
herring	*Hering* m.
hi	*hallo*
high	*hoch*
high beams	*Fernlicht* n.
high school	*Gymnasium* n.
highchair	*Hochstuhl* m.
higher education institute	*Hochschule* f.
high-heeled shoes	*hochhackige Schuhe* pl.
highlighter	*Textmarker* m.
high-school diploma	*Abitur* n.
highway	*Landstraße* f.
to hike	*wandern*
his	*sein*
historic	*historisch*
to hitchhike	*trampen*
hockey	*Hockey* n.
homesickness	*Heimweh* n.
home(ward)	*nach Hause*
homework	*Hausaufgaben, Schularbeit* f.
honeymoon	*Flitterwochen* pl.
horse, steed	*Ross* n.
hospital	*Krankenhaus* n.
hot	*heiß*
hotel	*Hotel* n.
hour	*Stunde* f.
house	*Haus* n.
how	*wie*
humid	*feucht*
hundred	*hundert*

hunger	*Hunger* m.
hunt	*Jagd* f.
to hunt	*jagen*
to hurt	*weh tun*
hyperactive	*aufgedreht*
I	*ich*
ice; ice cream	*Eis* n.
identification	*Ausweis* m.
immediately	*sofort*
impatient	*ungeduldig*
in cash	*bar*
included	*inbegriffen*
incoming mail, inbox	*Posteingang* m.
Indian (East)	*Inder* m., *Inderin* f.
industry	*Industrie* f.
infected	*infiziert*
inhaler	*Inhalationsapparat* m.
injection, shot	*Injektion, Spritze* f.
to injure	*verletzen*
inn	*Gasthof* m.
innovative	*innovativ*
insomnia	*Schlaflosigkeit* f.
insurance	*Versicherung* f.
to insure	*versichern*
to interest	*interessieren (sich)*
interest rate	*Zinssatz* m.
interesting	*interessant*
Internet	*Internet* n.
interrupted	*unterbrochen*
interview	*Vorstellungsgespräch* n.
to introduce	*vorstellen*
introduction	*Vorstellung* f.
iodine	*Jod* n.
it	*es*
it can be	*es lässt sich*
Italian	*italienisch*
Italian (person)	*Italiener* m., *Italienerin* f.
jacket	*Jacke* f.
jam, marmelade	*Marmelade* f.
January	*Januar* m.
Japanese	*japanisch*
Japanese (person)	*Japaner* m., *Japanerin* f.
jaw	*Kiefer* m.
jeans	*Jeans* pl.
jet lag; time change	*Zeitumstellung* f.

jewelry	*Schmuck* m.
job	*Job* m.
jobless	*arbeitslos*
to jog	*joggen*
joking, playful	*scherzhaft*
juice	*Saft* m.
July	*Juli* m.
June	*Juni* m.
hoodie	*Kapuzenpulli* m.
keyboard	*Tastatur* f.
kick	*Tritt* m.
kilogram	*Kilo* n., *Kilogramm* n.
kilometer	*Kilometer* m.
kind, friendly	*freundlich*
kindergarten	*Kindergarten* m.
to kiss	*küssen*
kitchen	*Küche* f.
knee	*Knie* n.
knife	*Messer* n.
to know	*wissen*
to know, be acquainted	*kennen*
lad, boy	*Knabe* m.
lake	*See* m.
lamb	*Lamm* n.
to land	*landen*
lane	*Gasse* f.
laptop	*Laptop* m.
last name	*Nachname* m.
late	*spät*
to laugh	*lachen*
laundry, laundromat	*Wäscherei* f.
laundry service	*Wäschedienst* m.
lawyer	*Rechtsanwalt* m., *Rechtsanwältin* f.
laxative	*Abführmittel* n.
lazy	*faul*
to lead	*führen*
to leave (behind)	*hinterlassen*
left	*links*
leg	*Bein* n.
lemon	*Zitrone* f.
lemonade	*Limonade* f.
less, fewer	*weniger*
to let	*lassen*
letter	*Brief* m.
lettuce	*Kopfsalat* m.

to lie down	*hinlegen (sich)*
light blue	*hellblau*
light, easy, mild	*leicht*
to like	*gern haben*
to like, want to	*mögen*
likeable	*sympathisch*
lime	*Limone* f.
to limp	*hinken*
lip	*Lippe* f.
liqueur	*Likör* m.
liter	*Liter* n.
little (amount)	*wenig*
a little, a bit	*bisschen (ein)*
little bird	*Vöglein* n.
little, small	*klein*
loaf	*Laib* m.
loan	*Darlehen* n.
lobster	*Hummer* m.
local anesthesia	*örtliche Betäubung* f.
local call	*Ortsgespräch* n.
loneliness	*Einsamkeit* f.
lonely	*einsam*
long	*lang*
long-distance call	*Ferngespräch* n.
to look at, watch	*ansehen (sich)*
to look for, seek	*suchen*
loose, slack	*lose*
to lose	*verlieren*
to love	*lieben*
lover	*Geliebte* m./f.
low	*niedrig*
lunch	*Mittagessen* n.
luxury car	*Luxuswagen* m.
lyrical	*lyrisch*
mad	*böse*
maid	*Dienstmädchen* n.
mail, post office	*Post* f.
mailbox	*Briefkasten* m.
main course	*Hauptgericht* n.
major, main subject (academic)	*Hauptfach* n.
to make, do	*machen*
mall, shopping center	*Einkaufszentrum* n.
man, husband	*Mann* m.
manager	*Manager* m., *Managerin* f.
many	*viele*

map	*Landkarte* f.
March	*März* m.
market	*Markt* m.
to marry	*heiraten*
to matriculate	*immatrikulieren*
May	*Mai* m.
may, to be allowed	*dürfen*
meal	*Mahlzeit* f.
to mean	*bedeuten*
mean, nasty	*gemein*
meat	*Fleisch* n.
mechanic	*Mechaniker* m., *Mechanikerin* f.
mechanical	*mechanisch*
medication	*Medikament* n.
medium (size)	*mittelgroß*
medium well/rare (meat)	*halb durchgebraten*
meeting	*Treffen* n.
men's clothing	*Männerkleidung* f.
menu	*Speisekarte* f.
message	*Nachricht* f.
Mexican	*mexikanisch*
Mexican (person)	*Mexikaner* m., *Mexikanerin* f.
midnight	*Mitternacht* f.
mild	*mild*
milk	*Milch* f.
milliliter	*Milliliter* n.
million	*Million* f.
mine, my	*mein*
mineral water	*Mineralwasser* n.
minimum wage	*Mindestlohn* m.
miniskirt	*Minirock* m.
minute	*Minute* f.
mittens	*Fausthandschuhe* pl.
mobile telephone	*Mobiltelefon* n.
molar	*Backenzahn* m.
Monday	*Montag* m.
money	*Geld* n.
money order	*Postanweisung* f.
monitor, screen	*Monitor* m., *Bildschirm* m.
moped	*Moped* n.
more	*mehr*
morning	*Morgen* m.
mother	*Mutter* f.
mouse	*Maus* f.
mouth	*Mund* m.

movie theater	*Kino* n.
Mr., sir	*Herr* m.
much	*viel*
mugging	*Straßenraub* m.
museum	*Museum* n.
mushroom	*Pilz* m.
music	*Musik* f.
mussels	*Muscheln* pl.
must, to have to	*müssen*
mustard	*Senf* m.
my, mine	*mein*
naive	*naiv*
name	*Name* m.
napkin	*Serviette* f.
national	*national*
nature	*Natur* f.
near	*nah*
neck	*Hals* m.
neckerchief, scarf	*Halstuch* n.
necklace	*Halskette* f.
to need	*brauchen*
negative	*negativ*
nephew	*Neffe* m.
nervous	*nervös*
new	*neu*
never	*nie, niemals*
newspaper	*Zeitung* f.
newspaper stand	*Zeitungskiosk* m.
next	*nächste*
next to	*neben*
niece	*Nichte* f.
night	*Nacht* f.
nine	*neun*
nineteen	*neunzehn*
ninety	*neunzig*
no	*nein*
no, not a, not any	*kein*
no one	*niemand*
no vacancy	*belegt*
nonsense	*Unsinn* m.
noodles	*Nudeln* pl.
noon	*Mittag* m.
north	*Norden* m.
nose	*Nase* f.
not	*nicht*

notebook	*Heft* n.
nothing	*nichts*
November	*November* m.
number	*Nummer* f.
nurse	*Krankenpfleger* m., *Krankenschwester* f.
occupation	*Beruf* m.
October	*Oktober* m.
offensive	*offensiv*
oh, alas	*ach*
old	*alt*
on	*auf*
on the way	*unterwegs*
once	*einmal*
one	*eins*
one another, each other	*einander*
one, someone	*man*
one-way street	*Einbahnstraße* f.
onion	*Zwiebel* f.
only	*nur*
open	*offen*
to open	*aufmachen, öffnen*
open-minded	*aufgeschlossen*
opera	*Oper* f.
optimist	*Optimist* m.
or	*oder*
orange	*Apfelsine* f., *Orange*, f.
orange (color)	*orange*
orchestra	*Orchester* n.
to order	*bestellen*
organ (musical instrument)	*Orgel* f.
our	*unser*
out, from	*aus*
outgoing, sociable	*kontaktfreudig*
over there	*dort drüben*
package	*Paket* n.
pajamas	*Schlafanzug* m.
panties	*Schlüpfer* m.
pants	*Hose* f.
pantyhose, tights	*Strumpfhose* f.
paper	*Papier* n.
paper clip	*Büroklammer* f.
park	*Park* m.
to park	*parken*
parking lot	*Parkplatz* m.
parsley	*Petersilie* f.

party, celebration	*Party* f., *Fest* n.
to pass	*überholen*
passenger	*Passagier* m.
passport	*Pass* m.
passport control (immigration)	*Passkontrolle* f.
pastry shop	*Konditorei* f.
patient	*geduldig*
patriotic	*patriotisch*
to pay	*zahlen*
to pay for	*bezahlen*
peace	*Frieden* m.
peach	*Pfirsich* m.
peanut	*Erdnuss* f.
pear	*Birne* f.
peas	*Erbsen* pl.
pen (fountain)	*Füller* m.
pencil	*Bleistift* m.
pendant	*Anhänger* m.
penicillin	*Penizillin* n.
pepper	*Pfeffer* m.
per	*pro*
perfect	*perfekt*
performance	*Aufführung* f., *Vorstellung* f., *Vorführung* f.
perfume	*Parfüm* n.
permanent, perm	*Dauerwelle* f.
person	*Person* f.
pessimist	*Pessimist* m.
pet	*Haustier* n.
pharmacist	*Apotheker* m., *Apothekerin* f.
photo	*Foto* n.
piano	*Klavier* n.
picture postcard	*Ansichtskarte* f.
pie	*Obstkuchen* m.
piece	*Stück* n.
pig	*Schwein* n.
pill	*Pille* f.
pillow	*Kissen* n.
pilot	*Pilot* m., *Pilotin* m.
pin (decorative)	*Anstecknadel* f.
pink	*rosa*
plate	*Teller* m.
to play	*spielen*
please	*bitte*
plum	*Pflaume* f.
plumber	*Klempner* m., *Klempnerin* f.

Pole, Polish	*Pole* m., *Polin* f.
police	*Polizei* m.
police officer	*Polizist* m., *Polizistin* f.
police station	*Polizeistation* f.
political	*politisch*
popular	*populär*
pork	*Schweinefleisch* n.
portable	*tragbar*
positive	*positiv*
post office	*Post* f., *Postamt* n.
postage	*Porto* n.
postage due	*Nachgebühr* f.
postage stamp	*Briefmarke* f.
postcard	*Postkarte* f.
pot, jar	*Topf* m.
potato	*Kartoffel* f.
poultry	*Geflügel* n.
pound (weight/money)	*Pfund* n.
to pour	*gießen*
pregnant	*schwanger*
prescription	*Rezept* n.
present, gift	*Geschenk* n.
presentation, performance	*Vorführung* f., *Vorstellung* f.
president	*Präsident* m., *Präsidentin* f.
pretty, nice	*schön*
print, printing	*Druck* m.
printer	*Drucker* m.
problem	*Problem* n.
professor	*Professor* m., *Professorin* f.
to prove	*beweisen*
public	*öffentlich*
pudding	*Pudding* m.
pupil	*Schüler* m.
quark, curd cheese	*Quark* m.
quarter	*Viertel* n.
quiet, calm	*ruhig*
rain	*Regen* m.
to rain	*regnen*
raincoat	*Regenmantel* m.
rainy	*regnerisch*
raise, salary increase	*Lohnerhöhung* f.
rape	*Vergewaltigung* f.
rare (meat)	*englisch gebraten*
raspberry	*Himbeere* f.
rat	*Ratte* f.

to react	*reagieren*
to read	*lesen*
receipt	*Quittung* f.
to receive	*empfangen*
receiver (phone)	*Hörer* m.
reception (desk)	*Rezeption* f.
receptionist (hotel)	*Empfangschef* m., *Empfangsdame* f.
recipient, addressee	*Empfänger* m., *Empfängerin* f.
red	*rot*
registered	*eingeschrieben*
regular gas	*Normalbenzin* n.
relative	*relativ*
to remain, stay	*bleiben*
remedy	*Heilmittel* n.
remote, (away) from	*entfernt*
repair	*Reparatur* f.
to repair	*reparieren*
to repeat	*wiederholen*
to replace	*ersetzen*
republic	*Republik* f.
reservation	*Reservierung* f.
reserved, guarded	*zurückhaltend*
restaurant	*Restaurant* n.
resume	*Lebenslauf* m.
rhythmic	*rhythmisch*
ribbon	*Band* n.
rice	*Reis* m.
right	*rechts*
ring	*Ring* m.
to ring	*klingeln*
to rinse	*spülen, durchspülen*
to rinse out	*ausspülen*
roast beef	*Roastbeef* n., *Rinderbraten* m.
roll	*Brötchen* n.
to roller-skate	*Rollschuh laufen*
romantic	*romantisch*
room	*Zimmer* n.
root canal	*Wurzelbehandlung* f.
rose	*Rose* f.
round-trip airline ticket	*Hin- und Rückflugkarte* f.
to row	*rudern*
to run	*laufen*
runny nose	*laufende Nase*
Russian	*Russe* m., *Russin* f.
rye bread	*Roggenbrot* n.

sad	*traurig*
to sail	*segeln*
salad	*Salat* m.
salary	*Lohn* m.
salt	*Salz* n.
sandals	*Sandalen* pl.
Saturday	*Samstag* m., *Sonnabend* m.
saucer	*Untertasse* f.
sausage	*Wurst* f.
to save	*sparen*
savings account	*Sparkonto* n.
savings bank	*Sparkasse* f.
to say	*sagen*
to say *du* to (address informally)	*duzen*
to say *Sie* to (address formally)	*siezen*
scanner	*Scanner* m.
scarf, muffler	*Schal* m.
school	*Schule* f.
sea	*See* f.
seasick	*seekrank*
seasickness	*Seekrankheit* f.
seat	*Platz* m.
to seat (oneself)	*setzen (sich)*
secretary	*Sekretär* m., *Sekretärin* f.
security check	*Sicherheitskontrolle* f.
to see	*sehen*
to sell	*verkaufen*
to send	*senden*
sender	*Absender* m.
September	*September* m.
serious	*ernst*
service	*Service* m.
service; call to the waiter	*Bedienung* f.
seven	*sieben*
seventeen	*siebzehn*
seventy	*siebzig*
to shave (oneself)	*rasieren (sich)*
shawl	*Schultertuch* n.
she, her, it (f.)	*sie* sing.
sheep	*Schaf* n.
shirt	*Hemd* n.
shoe size	*Schuhgröße* f.
shoes	*Schuhe* pl.
shop	*Laden* m.
to shop	*einkaufen*

short (time, length, distance)	*kurz*
shot	*Schuss* m.
should	*sollen*
shoulder	*Schulter* f.
to show	*zeigen*
shower	*Dusche* f.
shuttle bus	*Pendelbus* m.
shy	*schüchtern*
sick	*krank*
to sign	*unterschreiben*
to sing	*singen*
sinusitis	*Sinusitis* f.
sister	*Schwester* f.
to sit down	*hinsetzen (sich)*
six	*sechs*
sixteen	*sechzehn*
sixty	*sechzig*
size	*Größe* f.
to ski	*Ski laufen*
ski jacket	*Skijacke* f.
skirt	*Rock* m.
to sleep	*schlafen*
slip	*Unterrock* m.
sloppy	*schlampig*
slow	*langsam*
to slow down	*verlangsamen*
small, little	*klein*
smart, clever	*klug*
to smoke	*rauchen*
snack	*Snack* m.
snack bar	*Schnellimbiss* m.
to sneeze	*niesen*
to snow	*schneien*
so long, bye	*tschüs*
soap	*Seife* f.
soccer	*Fußball* m.
socialistic	*sozialistisch*
sock	*Socke* f.
sofa	*Sofa* n.
softener (fabric)	*Weichspülmittel* n.
software	*Software* f.
solid	*solid*
someone	*jemand*
something	*etwas*
son	*Sohn* m.

sophisticated	*kultiviert*
sorrow	*Leid* n.
soup	*Suppe* f.
sour cream	*Sauerrahm* m.
south	*Süden* m.
Spaniard	*Spanier* m., *Spanierin* f.
sparkling water	*Selterswasser* n.
sparkling wine, champagne	*Sekt* m.
to speak	*sprechen*
speed limit	*Geschwindigkeitsbeschränkung* f.
to spend (money)	*ausgeben*
spider	*Spinne* f.
spinach	*Spinat* m.
spoon	*Löffel* m.
sports coat	*Sakko* m.
spouse	*Gatte* m., *Gattin* f.
spring	*Frühling* m.
to stand back	*zurückbleiben*
staple	*Heftklammer* f.
stapler	*Hefter* m.
starch	*Stärke* f.
statistic	*Statistik* f.
steak	*Steak* n.
steering wheel	*Lenkrad* n.
still	*noch*
stocking	*Strumpf* m.
stomach	*Magen* m.
stomachache	*Magenschmerzen* pl.
stone, rock	*Stein* m.
to stop, cease	*aufhören*
stopover	*Zwischenlandung* f.
store	*Geschäft* n.
storm	*Gewitter* n.
stormy	*stürmisch*
straight ahead	*geradeaus*
stranger	*Fremde* m./f.
strawberry	*Erdbeere* f.
street	*Straße* f.
strict	*strikt*
to stroll	*bummeln, spazieren*
strong	*stark*
student	*Student* m., *Studentin* f.
studious	*lerneifrig*
stupid	*dumm*
style	*Stil* m.

subject (school)	*Fach* n.
subtitle	*Untertitel* m.
subway	*U-Bahn* f.
to suffer	*leiden*
sugar	*Zucker* m.
suit	*Anzug* m.
sum	*Summe* f.
summer	*Sommer* m.
sunburn	*Sonnenbrand* m.
Sunday	*Sonntag* m.
sunglasses	*Sonnenbrille* f.
sunny	*sonnig*
superhighway, expressway	*Autobahn* f.
supermarket	*Supermarkt* m.
surname	*Familienname* m.
sweater	*Pullover* m.
Swede	*Schwede* m., *Schwedin* f.
to swim	*schwimmen*
swimming pool	*Schwimmbad* n.
Swiss	*Schweizer* m., *Schweizerin* f.
symphony	*Sinfonie* f.
system	*System* n.
table	*Tisch* m.
tablet, pill	*Tablette* f.
to take a shower	*duschen (sich)*
to take off (aircraft)	*starten*
to take off, take from	*abnehmen*
tan	*sonnengebräunt*
taxi	*Taxi* n.
taxi stand	*Taxistand* m.
tea	*Tee* m.
teacher	*Lehrer* m., *Lehrerin* f.
teeth cleaning	*Zahnreinigung* f.
telephone	*Telefon* n.
telephone book	*Telefonbuch* n.
television program	*Fernsehsendung* f.
television set	*Fernsehapparat* m.
temporary	*vorübergehend*
ten	*zehn*
tennis	*Tennis* n.
tent	*Zelt* n.
to thank	*danken*
that	*jener, jene, jenes*
that (conjunction)	*dass*
the (f.)	*die*

the (m.)	*der*
the (n.), that	*das*
theater	*Theater* n.
theft	*Diebstahl* m.
their	*ihr*
there	*da, dort*
there is/are	*es gibt*
they	*sie pl.*
thief	*Dieb* m.
thin	*dünn*
thirst	*Durst* m.
thirteen	*dreizehn*
thirty	*dreißig*
this	*dieser, diese, dieses*
thousand	*tausend*
three	*drei*
through	*durch*
to throw up	*erbrechen (sich)*
thumb	*Daumen* m.
to thunder	*donnern*
Thursday	*Donnerstag* m.
tie	*Schlips* m.
tie clip	*Krawattenhalter* m.
time	*Zeit* f.
tip, gratuity	*Trinkgeld* n.
tired	*müde*
to	*zu*
tobacco shop	*Tabakwarenhändler* m.
today	*heute*
toe	*Zeh* m.
toilet, restroom	*Toilette* f.
tomato	*Tomate* f.
tomorrow	*morgen*
tooth	*Zahn* m.
toothache	*Zahnweh* n.
toothbrush	*Zahnbürste* f.
torrent	*Strom* m.
torte, tart, flan	*Torte* f.
total	*total*
total, amount	*Betrag* m.
towel	*Handtuch* n.
traffic jam	*Verkehrsstau* m.
traffic light	*Verkehrsampel* f.
train	*Zug* m.
train platform	*Bahnsteig* m.

train schedule	*Zugfahrplan* m.
train station	*Bahnhof* m.
transportation	*Transport* m.
traveler's check	*Reisescheck* m.
tray	*Tablett* n.
trillion	*Billion* f.
truck	*Lastwagen* m.
trumpet	*Trompete* f.
T-shirt	*T-Shirt* n.
Tuesday	*Dienstag* m.
turkey	*Truthahn* m.
to turn (automobile)	*einbiegen*
to turn off	*abschalten*
to turn on	*anschalten*
turn signal	*Blinker* m.
tuxedo	*Smoking* m.
twelve	*zwölf*
twenty	*zwanzig*
two	*zwei*
typewriter	*Schreibmaschine* f.
ugly	*hässlich*
umbrella	*Regenschirm* m.
uncle	*Onkel* m.
under	*unter*
undershirt	*Unterhemd* n.
to understand	*verstehen*
underwear	*Unterwäsche* f.
to undress (oneself)	*ausziehen (sich)*
university	*Universität* f.
until	*bis*
vanilla	*Vanille* f.
vase	*Vase* f.
veal	*Kalbfleisch* n.
vegetarian	*Vegetarier* m.
very	*sehr*
violin	*Geige* f.
visa	*Visum* n.
to visit	*besuchen*
volleyball	*Volleyball* m.
waiter, server	*Kellner* m., *Kellnerin* f.
wake-up call	*Weckanruf* m.
wallet	*Brieftasche* f.
to want	*wollen*
wardrobe	*Kleiderschrank* m.
warm	*warm*

to wash (oneself)	*waschen (sich)*
washing machine	*Waschmaschine* f.
to watch televeision	*fernsehen*
water	*Wasser* n.
to water ski	*Wasserski laufen*
we	*wir*
weak	*schwach*
weather	*Wetter* n.
website	*Website* f.
wedding	*Hochzeit* f.
wedding anniversary	*Hochzeitstag* m.
wedding ring	*Ehering* m.
Wednesday	*Mittwoch* m.
week	*Woche* f.
weight	*Gewicht* n.
to weigh	*wiegen*
well	*wohl*
well, fountain	*Brunnen* m.
well done (meat)	*durchgebraten*
west	*Westen* m.
what	*was*
when	*wann*
whenever, if	*wenn*
where	*wo*
where (to)	*wohin*
whether, if	*ob*
which	*welcher, welche, welches*
white	*weiß*
who	*wer*
whole-wheat bread	*Vollkornbrot* n.
why	*warum*
Wi-Fi, WLAN	*WLAN* n.
window	*Fenster* n.
windshield	*Windschutzscheibe* f.
windshield wiper	*Scheibenwischer* m.
windy	*windig*
wine	*Wein* m.
wineglass	*Weinglas* n.
winter	*Winter* m.
wisdom tooth	*Weisheitszahn* m.
with	*mit*
with it	*damit*
without	*ohne*
woman, wife	*Frau* f.
women's clothing	*Frauenkleidung* f.

work, job	*Arbeit* f.
worried	*besorgt*
to wound	*verwunden*
wrinkles	*Falten* pl.
wrist	*Handgelenk* n.
to write	*schreiben*
writer	*Schriftsteller* m., *Schriftstellerin* f.
yellow	*gelb*
yes	*ja*
yogurt	*Joghurt* m.
you (formal)	*Sie*
you (pl., informal)	*ihr*
you (sing., informal)	*du*
your (*du*)	*dein*
your (*ihr*)	*euer*
your (*Sie*)	*Ihr*
zip code	*Postleitzahl* f.
zoo	*Zoo* m.

Index